The RFP Success™ Book

Do Better. Win More.

Girl With Drive Press
125 Park Ave., 25th fl
New York, NY 10017
www.girlwithdrive.press

Ordering Information:
Quantity sales. Special discounts are available on quantity purchases by corporations, associations, and others. For details, contact the publisher at the address above.

First Printing, 2018

ISBN 978-1-7322841-0-4

Printed in the United States of America

The RFP Success™ Book

Do Better. Win More.

Lisa Rehurek

Girl With Drive Press
New York

Contents

Foreword

I answered my first RFP in 1997, and I thought this was going to be the easiest way to sell our products. Just answer "YES" to all the questions because if we didn't have the capabilities we would deal with that after we won the business. Well, guess what...everyone else did the same thing so nothing set us apart from the competition. I didn't realize, at the time, that everyone just used the RFP to basically repeat all the information you could find out about our business from our website or our customers. When we analyzed our win rate and learned it was less than 20%, I discovered we were taking the time to participate and answer these long exhaustive RFPs, but we weren't setting ourselves apart from anyone else.

One of the most significant changes we made is what Lisa states right up front in her book regarding myths. We subscribed to Myth #6, "The RFP response is all about me and my company and our product/service." Thinking back to how we responded, we were great at telling you plenty of times in the proposal about every product we had and how you could use ALL of them. We never spent the time to explain how we were going to solve the problem statement that was being asked within the RFP. We lost so much in future work because we never took the time to explain our value and exactly how we had solutions for their needs. We could have easily just come right out and said what we could do, but we always seemed to want to hide behind all our accomplishments and the number of products we had in our tool kit. It seems so simple but for some reason it is hard to just state the obvious.

I have known Lisa for 30 plus years and what she has always recognized is to stop over complicating whatever it is you are doing, start thinking simplistically, and whatever you do, do it better next time. In the RFP Success™ Book, this is exactly the concept that will get you on the road to having enormous success in responding to a RFP. Think about one of the very important tasks Lisa tells us to perform...read the entire proposal. What a concept! Reading the proposal in its entirety will help you understand the 30,000 foot view of what solution they are needing. Like I said earlier, we weren't even sharing a solution we were just telling you the same thing about our company and products repeatedly just with different words.

Embrace the RFP...okay, not really the most innovative or sexy topic you will ever hear; however it's truly amazing how many companies have full RFP teams dedicated to just answering RFPs and yet they really don't embrace it as a full-on sales opportunity. You will hear that concept through this book and it is so true. Even just the tip from Lisa on remembering that there really is a "live" person on the other end of the RFP that you are talking directly to can swing the document from just being a bunch of information to something that is more conversational and tells the story of your solution. Once I decided that I was going to use the RFP just like it is a live presentation, it changed the entire way I responded. I immediately saw an increase in not only the number of RFPs that we were winning, but the number that we were being asked back to as the final group. We added personality and a more personal style of speaking to our answers. There was more warmth and passion in our responses and we were told that was why we were often asked back into the final group.

Speaking of being told why we won....Lisa and I were having dinner one night and we were talking about ways to set yourself apart in the RFP process (yes, I know that sounds like we have really "fun" dinners talking about RFPs, but it was over Martinis so that made it all better!). As I mentioned to her, one of the things I had started doing over the past 10 years was trying to find out why we didn't get selected in the process; understanding how our competitors set themselves apart from us so we could know how to grow in the future. That was helpful, but even more helpful was asking our customers why we did win the work. I found this to be very interesting. For many it was because they felt we "embraced" the process and respected them as the customer by spending time trying to explain our solutions that fit their challenge(s). Well isn't that funny! If we would have only listened to our customers earlier, I wouldn't have had to spend the last 30 years trying to perfect my RFP process!

There are so many tools and processes you will be able to take from Lisa and her long success that I know you are going to enjoy this journey. Embrace it and then listen to all the things you need to Stop-Start-Avoid-Elevate!

Robin Merritt
Global Senior Vice President
Axsium Group

Why Should I Read This Book About RFPs?

"Lisa! Who the heck's got time to read a book about RFPs?!"

That's what I envision people saying to me when I show them this book, and that's certainly what I first asked myself when I embarked on this journey of writing this book. But as I continue to get clients who need help, a *lot* of help, I realized that if you bid on RFPs, you *need* to take the time to read this book. Plain and simple.

I've made it easy to do that, so you don't feel like it's this long, arduous book that you don't get any take-aways from. This book is chock *full* of strategies and takeaways, one simple chapter at a time. In fact, that's all this book is.

I wrote this book because it breaks my heart to see the same unnecessary mistakes made over and over again. I review hundreds of proposals a year and each time my inner dialogue says something like, "Crap!! AGAIN?!!" (lovingly, of course). I talk to buyers and they tell me the same stories of what drives them absolutely nuts. I know there's a lot of frustration for those of you bidding on RFPs, but you're making simple mistakes and we need to fix that now!

Another reason I wrote this book is because I know that not everyone can afford to hire help. Plus, I want reminders in the hands of the people that do hire my company, so they continue to use these strategies and ideas to improve their RFP results.

Responding to an RFP is not a one-dimensional activity. It requires up front strategy, a built-in efficient process, the right mindset, the ability to draw in your audience, the ability to connect with your buyer(s), the right team members, and some personality (what *what*?! Personality?? YES!). It starts long before you get the RFP in your hands and continues long after you win or lose a specific proposal. The more you embrace this universal approach to responding to RFPs, the more success you'll have.

Bidding on RFPs can be a crapshoot, no matter how much homework you've done, no matter how strong you've connected with the buyers, no matter how strong your foundation.

Let me tell you a story......

> *My team and I had a recent client who did everything right. They weren't well-versed in RFPs, but they had been working the relationship with a particular state agency, and they had contracts with sister departments. They were well-positioned. In addition, they got the RFP because the potential client sent it to them. That's a perfect set-up! They'd done so much right.*
>
> *The bad news was, their product didn't meet the requirements of the RFP. Our client reached out and asked a clarifying question, and the agency urged them to still bid. Together we made the strategic decision to move forward.*
>
> *In the end, they lost.*
>
> *A heartbreaking loss, with the feeling that it was all for nothing. Come to find out, the person they had the relationship with had an emergency and left the agency before the bids were reviewed. Without that advocate in their corner, my client was no longer well positioned.*

You are going to lose some, even if everything is lined up correctly.

And frankly, in the beginning you're going to lose a lot and it's going to be painful. It's like any sales strategy - until you really get acclimated to your market and the players, and get your internal processes and strategy down, your win percent is going to be lower. The more of these strategies that you incorporate over time, the higher your win percent will climb. You will learn what to bid on and what not to bid on; you'll write more impactfully; you'll submit better responses that come to life for your readers/buyers.

This book is filled with reality filled stories like from my colleague Amy Shuman (pg. 41) who runs a proposal team whose win rate is 70%! That's very high and very impressive. This after she has been in this position for a long time, developed amazing processes, and knows what she's doing. Learn from Amy!

Your goal is to create that same type of environment where you win a lot more than you lose. That doesn't happen overnight, and it takes work. And paying attention.

Let me tell you a happier story.....

> *A few months ago, a client made a strategic decision to respond to an RFP for an ongoing contract. The contract had been held by the same company for years. There was no indication that the client was unhappy with their current vendor. We knew it was an uphill battle.*
>
> *Strategically, this was a high-profile target for our client and after an open and honest discussion about how this fits into their overall business development strategy, they decided to bid. Knowing that they had less than a 30% chance to win and unseat that incumbent, they took our advice to be bold and brazen in their response.*
>
> *They weren't shy to state the obvious and talk about the fact that they would be a new, unknown entity; that transition is never fun, but would be well worth it because of the new value they would bring. They know themselves well, so we were able to put together a killer Proposal Promise, and their differentiators were spot on. They were able to show increased value without an increase in price. And guess what?*
>
> *They won! They took a few risks and it paid off.*

You can't make decisions like that lightly, and you can't make decisions like that by the seat of your pants. If you're playing this game, you've got to be all in, and play to win.

When I started working on RFPs thirty years ago, I had no idea how big of a business it was. My first introduction to RFPs was in the hotel industry, where we would have to respond to a relatively straight-forward request for availability, rates, and amenities. There wasn't a whole lot to it.

Ten years later, I went to work for a large global consulting firm and was introduced to a whole different type of RFP. I used to refer to it as the beastly bomb. You know the one.......*200+ pages, intense terms and conditions, arduous requirements, numerous forms to fill out, conflicting instructions*. I used to think these were the Worst. Things. Ever.

The first thing I learned is that an effective process was imperative. If I could put a consistent and efficient process into place, it would make responding so much easier. True, to some point, but there was a heck of a lot more lessons to learn.

Brevity.
Simplicity.
Humanity.
Paying attention.
Value. VALUE!
Relationships.
Positioning.
Discipline.
Strategy.
Sanity.
Personality.
Fun! For the love of Pete, have some FUN!

I changed my mindset from thinking of it as a task, to thinking of it as a sales opportunity.

The more we won, the more business we had, the faster we grew, the more people we employed, the more clients we helped. It became exciting because it was a very important role in the wheel of business success.

If you're in this space of responding to RFPs, my first challenge to you is to change your mindset. Throughout this book I'll be sharing tips and strategies to make responding much simpler and more effective. I'll be sharing different strategies for showcasing your company in the best light possible and suggesting ways to up-level your responses. But all of that is for nothing if you don't have the right mindset going into it.

Lastly, this isn't really a book at all.

All of these strategies become your individual check list, checking off what you currently do and adding the aspects that are missing from your organization's RFP process.

You don't have to implement everything at once. This "book" will be here waiting for you with reminders and loving nudges on how to make your next RFP better. (Read "better" as more profitable.)

In the end, when you have fully implemented all the strategies and create an RFP system that you actually use, you will be less stressed and have more "Yeses" to the RFPs you submit.

How do I know his to be true? Because I see my clients succeed daily with their RFP success. And with 30 years of experience behind me, I know these strategies work.

One more thing. Throughout the book, I'll reference additional resources that will help support you in implementing these strategies. Some of these resources are free as part of this book (The RFP Success™ Kit), while others are part of our paid training platform (The RFP Success™ Institute) for those of you who want to go further with us in your learning.

Now, let's get started.

Meet Reality Rich

I get it. The people on an RFP evaluation team seem like the Wizard of OZ: Big, scary, potentially life-shattering, vague as all get-out on what they really want and, most importantly, what makes them say "Yes!" to your company's RFP response.

But trust me, they are just people! And just like in the Wizard of Oz, once we demystify how an RFP evaluation team thinks and the realities of their struggles, you will begin to look at the RFP responses you submit in a whole new light.

To help us understand the other side of the table, meet my friend Reality Rich.

Reality Rich works for a State agency and wears multiple hats - one of which is helping to select vendors for different services that his agency buys. You'll find Reality Rich on RFP evaluation teams frequently because he's always offering to help, even if it's not his area of expertise. He's not the top dog decision maker, but he is most definitely an influencer.

As RFP writers, our goal is to:

- Get to know the likes and dislikes of Rich;
- Understand what stresses him out and what makes his job easier;
- Learn how he thinks, communicates, and learns;
- Get to know what matters to him when it comes to helping his organization succeed.

To do this we must get to know Reality Rich.

Our recon has told us that Reality Rich is what we call a Social Butterfly; this is his personality style (you'll learn more about personality styles on pg. 184). Rich loves to be social and meet new people, a bit of a party animal. Because of his social nature, he can appear to be unfocused and he gets bored very easily. If he knows and likes you, he'll be a great internal advocate for you with the rest of the buying team.

With this information in hand, we need to think about how we can make our RFPs optimal for him. Consider:

- He's going to be advocating for the person he knows and likes; how will you become that person? How will you build a relationship with Reality Rich?
- If you're not that person, how are you going to appeal to Reality Rich? Especially in competition with the other bidders who may be buddies with Reality Rich?
- He gets bored easily
- He isn't a technical expert, more a jack of all trades; high level thinker, visionary
- He's not a detail-oriented guy
- Reality Rich is a skimmer; he's the guy that is only going to read "above the fold"
- Reality Rich is a little "me" focused

Now that we know the basics of who Reality Rich is and why it matters to us, Reality Rich is going to join us throughout the book to remind us of the nuances of our relationships with the buyers who are releasing these RFPs.

Keep an eye out for Reality Rich along the way!

Chapter 1.

The Top Ten Myths That Are Causing You To Lose Too Many RFPs

There are a lot of pre-conceived notions about RFPs that I want to dispel, because having the right mindset when responding to RFPs is crucial. If you are afraid, frustrated or in avoidance, it will affect your ability to create the best response possible. And what a waste of time that would be!

MYTH #1:

RFPs are all about cost; low-cost always wins.

False!

We are evolving into a value-based culture, where it's less about the bottom-line cost and more about the value that you can bring to the organization.

Don't get me wrong, there are still RFPs that are set up to choose the low-cost bidder. But we're seeing those less and less as time goes on. Buyers have been bitten in the pattootie too many times and are learning the lesson that value matters more than cost.

MYTH #2:

You can never un-seat an incumbent

False! Is it harder? Yes. But if you have been working on building your relationship and you have good reason to believe you can provide better value, there is absolutely a chance to successfully un-seat an incumbent.

If you didn't read the introduction, go back and read my story about a recent client who did just that – unseated the incumbent.

Look, there is a chance that the client *loves* the incumbent. If you're the incumbent, you hope that's the case. But that's not always the case.

The biggest reason that it's hard to unseat an incumbent is that it's perceived as a lot of work to make that change.

Think about your own life – have you ever decided to switch insurance companies? Or tax accountants? What a pain in the arse. You've got to gather a bunch of annoying paperwork that, let's face it, probably isn't all that organized; you have to get to know and trust someone new (and more importantly, they have to get to know you, which takes time). In the end, a lot of times it's easier to stay with mediocre than it is to make a switch.

That means it's your job to show the RFP evaluators:

1. Why it's worth it, and
2. How you're going to make it easy for them

If you can accomplish those two things, your chance just went way up to getting the "Yes".

MYTH #3:

All we have to do is to submit a bid and we'll instantly get a $60 million piece of business.

False. Come on people, you're smarter than that! Sadly, I have experienced this in discussions with many of our potential clients. They get all starry-eyed with the dollar value of a certain bid. Don't fall into that trap, because if you can't deliver, you'll fall prey to the "Oprah's Favorite Things" phenomenon – too big too fast. And that, my friends, can lead to disaster.

It's also not likely that you'll go from zero to $60 million right out of the gate.

A potential client came to my team and I last year asking for help on a handful of RFPs that had hit their desk. Five, to be exact (that's pretty much a red flag right there!). Someone had told him that bidding on public sector RFPs was the way to get large, long-term contracts. He got excited.

He had zero strategy and no experience. ZERO! Because he wasn't willing to talk strategy, we declined the opportunity to work with him.

The saddest part of this was that all five of these RFPs were for different types of work. He was literally getting ready to start slinging darts at an unknown target.

We highly encouraged him to choose just one that was really in their lane, and focus their time, energy and resources on that one. We also highly encouraged him to take a big step back and create a business development strategy to support him in his bidding efforts going forward. At the time, he declined.

Unfortunately, he didn't heed our advice, he bid on all five, and lost all five. Ouch! That's a huge waste of time and resources, and it leaves a bitter taste.

On the positive side, he did learn his lessen and now we are working on developing a strategy for his company.

MYTH #4:

RFPs are a necessary evil.

Sort of True. Sort of False. But it's a bad way to look at it. PERIOD.

If you want to do business with the government or with certain corporate entities that rely on RFPs for their purchasing, then you are going to have to embrace the fact that this is how your target client buys. Plain and simple.

It goes back to your mindset. And it's a big shift. As long as you think of the RFP process as an icky task, it will be an icky task.

A RFP is no more than a sales opportunity.

You heard it in the introduction, and you'll hear it again at least a few times......a RFP is no more than a sales opportunity. It's a tool that your clients use to purchase products and services. And because of that, it's the avenue that you will need to use to make the sale.

Be the best you can be with it. Reality Rich can tell when you're treating it like an icky task.

MYTH #5:

We need to showcase ALL of our expertise in this one response.

FALSE! This is one of the biggest mistakes people make. They want to showcase all the great bells and whistles; expertise and knowledge; but this is a mistake. The evaluator can't possibly take all of that in. It's hard enough to review multiple responses for what they *did* ask for.

Stick to what they need now.

And once you have that piece of business, you can work on showing them what else you can offer. In a later chapter you'll get to read all about one of my first horror stories, where we inundated the client with so much information, they didn't even end up reviewing our proposal. That hurts.

Don't do that.

MYTH #6:

The RFP response is all about me and my company and our product/service.

False. Your response is all about *how you solve a problem* for your potential client; how you add value and how you provide that solution.

Stop making it all about you!

There will be an opportunity to talk about you. All RFPs have sections where they ask specifically about you, your history, your experience. Use that time to showcase your knowledge and expertise.

The rest of the time, your expertise and knowledge should be shining through based on how you showcase that you will provide the solution that your prospect is asking for. It doesn't have to be so overt.

It's is *not* about you.

MYTH #7:

The only reason a company or agency releases an RFP is to get free advice.

False. Well, mostly false. Does this happen? *Yes, unfortunately.* Will you always know when that's the case? *No.* But there are signs to look for to identify when they are just shopping for free advice.

Frankly, if you have done your homework up front, you'll likely know the answer to this.

There are also signs that you can look for in the RFP itself. Is the timeframe to respond super short? Is there an absence of Q&A time or bidder's conference? Are the questions asked in an odd way?

The more you know about your market and your industry, and the more experience you have with RFPs in your market, the easier these will be to spot. Plus, if you've been doing your job of connecting with this prospect on a regular basis, you'll know the answer.

MYTH #8:

RFPs are hard and boring.

False. This doesn't have to be the case! You'll hear me say this *so many times* throughout this book - there are human beings on the other side of your proposal; let them get to know your personality. Give them something enjoyable to read.

Just because the RFP itself is buttoned-up and boring doesn't mean your response needs to be.

When a client sends us an RFP to review that they are looking to bid on, we almost always have to read it several times. Why? Because it's boring. My team and I don't like boring. I have to put a lot of effort into reading those long, arduous RFPs to really comprehend what they're asking for. We do that because our clients are hiring us to do that, and because we care about giving them the best opportunity to succeed. I doubt that all the reviewers on the evaluation team are going to put in that kind of effort. Don't give them boring or you'll lose them. You have the power!

MYTH #9:

We just have to shut up and respond to their question.

False-ish. This is more of a subconscious belief than it is a conscious thought. There is a time and a place to really push back, to get clarification, to not make any assumptions.

If there is something you don't understand, ask. If the information is too ambiguous and they aren't willing to clarify, walk away. If they haven't asked the right question, be the expert and tell them what they don't know without giving away your "secret sauce." Don't just be status quo. You have to answer their question to meet the requirements, but it doesn't always have to end there if you're able to add additional, relevant (key!) input.

MYTH #10:

We need them more than they need us.

False. This is another underlying subconscious pattern that drives the way we approach our response. And frankly, it's a theme in sales in general. We are looking for a win-win relationship here – where they get the best solution to their need/want, and we are able to share our expertise and provide that solution in our ideal situation.

Reality Rich needs you. He needs the right solution so he is a hero to his boss. He doesn't want to screw up, so he's looking for the right solution.

Being confident in your offering will show in your response. And FYI, being fearful or desperate will show too.

MYTH #11:

All RFPs are written poorly.

True. Well, mostly true.

Okay, so this is not really a myth, it's actually quite true. We very rarely see a RFP that is well organized and well written. When we do, it's an opportunity for celebration, that's how rare it is.

However, consider this: The team that is tasked with releasing the RFP likely has a gazillion things that they are juggling. They have probably taken a prior RFP and repurposed it; or cut and paste from various RFPs to create something that will work. They are no doubt on a tight timeframe to get this thing out the door.

Having a little empathy for the folks on the other end of the RFP will go a long way to that mindset shift I keep talking about.

***

The moral of the story? These myths are all assumptions, and they can screw up your ability to own your space and to bid confidently. Your best bet is to rid yourself of these myths!

Chapter 2.

Why Overlooking The Basics Is Draining Your Bank Account

You've got to get the basics right. These are the things that so many companies skip over because they take time and effort; they take pre-planning; they take being proactive.

But the world of RFPs tends to be very reactive.

You want the competitive edge? Get proactive and get down to basics so you can start seeing more success!

2.1. Get Your Mind Out Of The Gutter

"We're going to kick this off by talking about your mindset. Deep, eh?"

There are continuous mindset issues that come into play with RFPs. Many of them are embedded in the myths we just talked about, but one that we haven't deep dived into yet is one of the most important mindset issues:

You have got to change your mindset from thinking of an RFP as a task, to thinking of it as a sales opportunity.

When you think of it as a task, it feels heavy. It feels like a "have to" rather than an exciting opportunity full of potential.

You also have to say "adios" to negative thoughts around RFPs. Now, I'm not saying you're never going to have a negative or frustrating moment. There's a difference between that moment in time, and a continuous mindset. Staying in that negative space keeps you down in that bottom-feeding slime. It will not only impact your overall attitude, it will impact others on the team.

Your mindset is nothing more than an attitude.

The clearer and cleaner your attitude, the clearer and cleaner the outcome.

2.2. Strategy Is The Golden Ticket

When you get yourself and your team into the right frame of mind, now it's time to set a strategy. Building the right strategy is one of the biggest basics, and it's one of the most over-looked. Very few of our clients have a solid strategy when they first contact us.

Look......

1. Hope is NOT a Strategy;
2. Blind bidding is NOT a Strategy;
3. Bidding on everything is NOT a Strategy.

Strategy lays the foundation, without it your efforts will be futile. Do not, and I repeat not, avoid your strategy!

All right, so we all know we need it, but what does it even mean to have a strategy? It means we create a map, a game plan, so we aren't blindly swimming in the wrong ocean full of sharks.

A strategy gives us direction, so we are focusing our time, attention and resources on the right thing.

Clients and colleagues tell us all the time that they need to be better at time management. As soon as I hear them say that, I know they don't have a strategy, or at the very least, they sure aren't following it.

Here's the deal.....

Have you ever gotten into your car for a road trip, driven to a new state thousands of miles away, without a map? Likely not, unless you weren't overly concerned with when or how you would get there. You'd use a map or a GPS to help guide you.

Would you build a house by just nailing a bunch of 2x4's together, pouring a little concrete wherever you thought it should go, and slapping some drywall up? NO! You'd need to draw up plans and build a solid foundation.

And so it is with a business.

Your business success depends on building a solid foundation, because without it you won't have a complete direction for where you're going or how you're going to get there.

Now, what does this have to do with RFPs? Everything!

Not only do you need to build a business strategy, but you need a bidding strategy.

For every. Single. Opportunity.

Your **business** strategy tells you who your target audience is, how much revenue you need, and how many clients you'll need to get to that number.

Your **bidding** strategy will tell you how you are going to differentiate yourself from the competition, how aggressive you will be in your offering, and what your proposal promise (more on all of this a bit later) is. It sets the entire stage and ensures everyone is on the same page.

Everything that you have done in your macro business strategy can now be parlayed into this micro bidding strategy. But if you haven't laid this foundation, how on earth will you know what you should and shouldn't bid on?

You feel like skipping over that bidding strategy? Sure, that's fine. Here are the results you're going to get time and time again:

1. Low win rate
2. Loss of money, time and energy
3. Increased stress, aggravation, and annoyance
4. Decreased revenue
5. Unmotivated team members

Bidding without a strategy is the equivalent of a cold response and experts say you have less than 5% chance of winning a cold response. I'd argue that it's less than 1%, but go ahead, try. Then kick yourself afterwards.

Instead, here's what I want for you:

- Ability to better manage resources
- Continue to improve your win %
- Waste less time
- Decrease stress, aggravation, frustration, annoyance among team members
- More money!

So, consider these questions for your bidding strategy:

1. How does this opportunity fit into your bigger revenue and client acquisition goals?
2. Is this one of your target clients?
3. What will your proposal promise be?
4. How will you stack up against the competition for this particular proposal?
5. How will you build trust and rapport?
6. How do you meet (or better, exceed) the requirements of the RFP?

There is nothing more frustrating than working your arse off, day and night, on a bid and then losing. Those losses take their toll on the business (read: bottom line dollars) and on the team (read: morale, fatigue, attitude, burnout).

You don't want that.

And I don't' want that for you.

To help you out, I have a downloadable **Bidding Strategy Checklist** for you at http://RFPSuccess.expert/kit.

Let's get further introduced to Reality Rich.

Reality Rich is reviewing several proposals for a current service-oriented RFP. He's got five proposals to review. He grabs the one at the top of the pile and starts reading.

First thing he notices is that they called him Rick. Oh no! Not off to a good start. One simple letter of the alphabet can have dire consequences. Despite the name snafoo, Reality Rich decides to keep reading.

He notices that this company isn't familiar to him, which is a little odd because he tends to know everyone in this particular space being the Social Butterfly that he is. He's curious, so onward with the reading.

As he gets into the meat of the proposal, he's confused. This company has no public sector experience, only commercial expertise. They don't seem to know the ins and outs of what it would take to contract with a government entity or even what challenges the public sector would have versus what they have experienced in the past. The whole thing just feels misaligned and off. There's nothing in their response that feels like he should be hiring them.

On the other side of the proposal is the company who prepared the response. For them, they have decided they want to start doing work in the public sector. This RFP came across their desk and it seemed to be in their wheelhouse of expertise, so they put together a proposal.

The problem is, they didn't do their homework. And they clearly didn't have a strategy. If they had done both, they could have showcased how their lack of public sector experience would not be a problem, and how they bring a fresh and innovative perspective. They could have addressed that elephant in the room and related their expertise to what Reality Rich and his agency ultimately needed.

If you don't know what you're aiming for, your client sure isn't going to know. And they are going to see right through you. They will feel the misalignment on their end. That strategy goes deep and wide to your business development success.

2.3 Know Who You Do (And Don't!) Want To Work With

Knowing who you do and don't want to work with is certainly part of your strategy, but it is important enough to warrant its own chapter because so many businesses – particularly small businesses – don't have a clear vision of this.

You do not (I repeat, NOT) have to work with everyone. In fact, everyone is *not* your target.

It's time to get a little selfish with it.

Be selfish with the type of person/company you *do* want to work with, so you're focusing on the best opportunities and letting go of the opportunities that drain you, frustrate you, and drive you crazy! Who do you *love* working with, and who do you *not* want to work with? This also goes for the type of projects that you want to work on.

To give you an example, we were working with a client who was focusing all their efforts on bidding on school district RFPs. They got a fair number of contracts, but the contracts were painful because the budgets were very small. Our client was exhausted because not only were their clients nickel and diming them, but our client needed so many of these contracts to stay afloat. We sat down with our client to define what they did and didn't want when it came to clients. And we were able to say that these school district contracts should only be about 20% of their business. We defined who would make up the other 80%, and they went to work focusing on winning that kind of business.

Want to know what questions to ask to get to the bottom of who you should be working with? Don't worry, I've got you covered in the RFP Success™ Kit.

It's okay to not want to work with everyone. If it's not a good fit for you, it isn't a good fit for them. We want a win-win all the way around.

As you work through this, *write it down!* It's proven that when we write things down versus just trying to go by what's in our head, the clearer we get. In fact, some fancy study tells us that we become 42% more likely to achieve our goals and dreams simply by writing them down on a regular basis. I'll take 42% more likelihood any day!

Here are some questions you want to start asking about your target client:

- Do they value outside help?
- What type of contractors/outsourced help (whatever it is that you offer) do they hire?
- What are their buying patterns?
- What do they value?
- What keeps them up at night?
- Are they innovative or more traditional?

You also want to make a list of what you do *not* want in a client. This is hard because it can feel judgmental. But the "don'ts" are just as important because we want the right alignment with the right client.

Keep tweaking this until you have a solid list of who your target client *is* and *is not*. Once you know this, you can start identifying actual targets, and prioritize them using the following method:

Green Light - high priority, hot prospects

Yellow Light - medium priority

Red Light - avoid!

This will become a guiding force as you get into your bidding strategy and bid decisions. You also want to make sure you share this with your team so they are on board.

And to keep you and your team on the same page, check out the **Target Client Questionnaire** in the RFP Success™ Kit (http://RFPSuccess.expert/kit). It is how I personally have organized my clients' target audiences for years.

2.4. Create A Process

There are two types of people in the world - those that love process, and those who despise it. Certainly, both have their merits.

If your internal processes are a mess, your response will be a mess. And no one's got time for a mess.

There's also a higher likelihood that you'll miss something and/or get disqualified. Remember, if the foundation of your home isn't level, the rest of the house is going to be a hot mess.

I'm not asking you to create over-complicated, 'processes-just-to-have-a-process', red-tape-laden processes. That's why many people hate processes.

Stop avoiding and underestimating a process! It will make life so much easier when responding to RFPs. And, it will set you up for success and growth. I promise.

Here are the types of processes that are imperative for ongoing success with RFPs.

The obvious:

- Bid/no-bid process
- Response management process
- Follow-up process

The not-so-obvious (or certainly under-used):

- Debrief process
- Tracking process
- Team process

You'll hear more about these processes in later chapters. Pick the area that you're weakest in and create a simple but effective process so everyone can be on the same page. Make a goal to implement one clean, simple process each quarter. Your team will love you for it!

If don't know where to start with creating or refining your processes, download our RFP Success™ Kit to get a copy of our **Process Audit Checklist** (http://RFPSuccess.expert/kit).

❑ Don't Just Take My Word For It...

Meet Amy Shuman. I met Amy back when I was in charge of proposals for a large corporate consulting firm and we'd attend the same conference together. We became fast friends even though we were competitors. Amy knows her stuff. She's been doing this for a long time and I was thrilled to get her input for this chapter.

***

The evolution of my proposal career mirrors that of a good proposal process: well-honed, refined, and revised on a continuous cycle of quality improvement. The RFP process was much simpler early in my career when a handful of individuals submitted two to three proposals each month. Fast forward 20 years and multiply by six. Now we have a well-oiled proposal machine with larger, multi-disciplinary teams submitting more than 12 proposals per month.

Our 70 percent win rate has remained fairly consistent through the years underscoring the importance of having an RFP process that is scalable, flexible and responsive.

That's pure bad-assery right here!

Improving the RFP process has been a process in and of itself. It is best described as a series of lessons learned, keeping in mind that any revision to the RFP process is designed with the same end result in mind: to produce a winning proposal. Lessons learned include:

1. **Respect the process.** *When the RFP process is valued from the top down, all others in the organization are willing to participate fully in the process. A RFP never seems to be released when there is a lull in workload. The opposite tends to be true. Countless evening and weekend hours are devoted to preparing a responsive, quality proposal. The RFP process works best when growing the firm is a core value at the heart of the organization.*

2. **Keep it simple.** *The traditional KISS rule applies here. The process must be simple enough to remain nimble. We have seen a drastic reduction in RFP response times. Tight turnarounds are the new norm. The process cannot hinder the ability to quickly respond.*

3. **Make it personal.** *The proposal process cannot override the importance of tailoring a proposal response to the specific needs of the prospective clients. The process must allow for and encourage a response to the RFP requirements that actually sees the prospective client's needs through the prospective client's eyes.*

In other words, use boilerplate language as a starting point, but rewrite each time to target the specific RFP.

4. **Cross train the team.** *Invariably the one person who knows how to use the org chart software will be out of the office when a last-minute change needs to be made. Plan ahead. Ensure there is always more than one person who knows how to perform a specific function.*

5. **Never ever skip the final review.** *Before any proposal is ever wrapped, packed and shipped, we flip through it page by page for a final review. This process has saved us from embarrassment and/or potential disqualification due to misspelled words on a cover page, incorrect RFP numbers, cost proposals with mathematical errors, missing pages, table of contents that does not align with page numbers, the list goes on.*

6. **Ship two days early.** *Weather happens. Unexpected delays happen. Plan for the inevitable every time without exception.*

7. **Learn from the losses.** *While it's never easy to lose, it is a great opportunity to make adjustments to the process to ensure future success. Many of the steps in our process are a direct result of a proposal loss. Additional reviewers are included to ensure all RFP requirements are addressed. Detailed RFP outlines are prepared to guide the proposal response. Evaluation materials are requested and shared with the team.*

8. **Celebrate the wins.** *The official client award notification announcing your firm as the successful bidder should trigger a celebration. Send a congratulatory email to those who worked on the proposal, announce the new contract firmwide and thank your proposal response team profusely. This is the direct result of the entire team's efforts and should always be celebrated.*

Amy Schuman
National Marketing Director
Myers and Stauffer LC

***

Thanks Amy! Great advice, and proof of what can happen when you embrace process. My personal favorite – Never, ever skip the final review. You'll read a horror story about that in a later chapter.

2.5. Leverage Time & Resources

There is so much to do when it comes to responding to RFPs.

How do you best leverage your time and resources to make the best showing in the allotted timeframe?

This is one of the most common questions that I personally get asked – "How do you get it all done in the allotted time?" There's never a time when a company tells me they have an over-abundance of staff and resources, or endless money to hire whoever and purchase whatever they want.

There are a few (not surprising) answers to this question:

1. Create a solid strategy (pg. 31);
2. Have the right processes (pg. 39);
3. Make sure you have the right people in the right roles (and yes, I talk about this too! Refer to the next chapter);
4. Get creative! Where can you get extra help? Who can you partner with? How can you put others to work for you?

I used to work for a large healthcare consulting firm. I was tasked with building the RFP function for a specialty practice whose business was 100% government contracts.

Twenty years ago, we didn't have a lot of the services that are now available to us to track opportunities. And early in the game, unless we were trolling each state agency website, we'd lose out on opportunities. This became a big problem.

The solution? We put all of our analysts to work by assigning each one of them a key state. We knew who our green-light state targets were and those were the states that got assigned a State Monitor.

It took the State Monitor maybe 30 minutes a week; but if I had tried to do that all on my own, I would have never had time.

We got creative and leveraged the rest of our team. And getting the technical analysts involved in business development was a win all the way around!

Today, there are services that will do this for you (like FindRFP.com or Bid-net.com), but those services aren't full-proof. So guess what? This process is STILL in play because of that; it's relevant and it works.

2.6. The Right Peeps Matter (No, Not Marshmallow Peeps)

Imagine that every time you hired someone, you'd get an extra $17,000. For each individual hire.

$17,000!

For some businesses, $17,000 is a part-time staff member;

For other businesses, $17,000 is a bonus pool for their five employees;

Heck, for some people, $17,000 is a nice down payment on a new car!

That's no small chunk of change, I don't care how big your business is. Because the bigger your business, the more that adds up. Now, I'm not going to give you $17,000, but get this...

The average cost of hiring the *wrong* employee is **$17,000** (according to some fancy-schmancy research conducted by Career Builder). And that's the quantifiable piece! That number doesn't even consider lost productivity or impact on morale of other employees. Plain and simple, hiring the wrong person can wreak havoc on your organization. While we don't presume anyone will get it right 100% of the time, we want to help minimize that as much as possible.

What impact would $17,000 make on your business? Or, $17,000 times five, or ten, depending on how many people are coming and going in a given year. The bigger the business, the more turnover, the higher that number. Would you change some of your habits to make that happen?

Plop this concept into the RFP world and it magnifies even more. Why? Because it's a direct link to a sales opportunity. Never mind the cost of recruiting, hiring, training, etc., think about the lost sales opportunities!

We hear it over and over, people are our number one asset in our businesses. Yet hiring is one of the most under-focused areas particularly for small business owners. Why? Because people are busy and overwhelmed and they don't necessarily have the expertise in hiring. This hinders our ability to be objective and hire for an overall appropriate fit.

You've got to create an honest and comprehensive job description. The emphasis is on 'honest' because we often fool ourselves into what this job requires. We don't want to 'scare people off' or 'come on too strong', so we soften and broaden the qualifications. We add all sorts of fluff words like "authentic," "positive," "go-getter." These unnecessary details water down the real message.

But heck yeah, we **do** want to scare people off! We want to be as upfront as possible so the *right* candidates apply for the position. The right people aren't going to scare that easily.

You've also got to assess the candidates' *objectively,* and that's tough. We are emotional beings. We meet someone, we like them based on personality or one piece of their experience, or even how well they interview. And we're human, we get sucked in. I'm not saying that experience and personality isn't important, it IS. But it's not necessarily objective.

Here are a handful of questions to ask yourself. When you can answer these impartially, it will increase long-term success for a candidate dramatically:

- How coachable are they? In other words, are they open to growth and development, or are they stuck in their ways?
- What type of rewards will drive them into action? For example, are they driven by money and recognition, or are they driven by being in service to others? And are the rewards aligned with their drive for this particular position?
- Are they an appropriate fit for the company culture? For example, are they very black and white and boxed in, where your culture is very open and flexible?

- How well will they fit with the needs of rest of the team and their supervisor? Are you hiring someone who is outgoing and friendly because everyone else is? Or do you have a team full of outgoing friendly folks, and you're missing that detail-oriented spoke?
- Is their behavioral style a good fit for the demands of the job? If the job requires someone that has a high level of urgency, but you hire someone that is slower-paced, more methodical, it's going to be a mis-match.

One of our clients was having a horrible time keeping their proposal coordinator. They were a small shop and the proposal coordinator was tasked with being a "jack-of-all-trades". It was the only full-time person on the proposal team. This position was turning over about every nine months, and they were settling for mediocre candidates because they were getting desperate each time there was turnover.

When we got involved, the first thing we did was review the job description.

It was all unclear fluff. Things like:

> *Must have good communication and writing skills (what does this even mean?)*
>
> *Be good at managing their time (again, what does this REALLY mean?)*
>
> *Be a team player (there are different ways to be a team player, believe me)*

It continued with asking for a high level of competency in certain computer programs; it spoke to certain types of experience.

Yes, all important. What was missing is that it didn't address the needs of the job on a day-to-day basis.

We got crystal clear on what the output needed to be in this position and what work pace the job required. We re-wrote the job description and three things happened (check out our before and after versions in the RFP Success™ Institute):

1. *Our client realized that they were looking for a unicorn; there was no way they could fit all those requirements into just one position;*

2. *We reorganized the position and created the right type of position and the right description;*

3. *They started getting a whole different type of applicant and had multiple highly qualified finalists.*

They have now had their proposal coordinator for 18 months and are adding another person to the team. They've saved enough money in those turnover costs and in winning more RFPs because of more stability in that role that they can afford to bring on another team member.

That's a great win!

You're going to hear more about hiring from hiring expert Talmar Anderson on pg. 72. And if you're not good at writing job descriptions, let me tell you, you're not alone. We cover this in depth in the RFP Success™ Institute for just that reason (http://RFPSuccessInstitute.com).

Now that you have the foundation laid, there's a couple of other "no brainer" things that you need to do.

2.7. Read The RFP Before You Decide To Bid. Without Delay.

Seriously. Read the RFP. All the way through.

"Way to state the obvious, Lisa!"

You'd be shocked at how many people hire us, pay a non-refundable deposit, and then tell us they haven't even read the RFP. And immediately we find something that will prevent them from bidding.

It doesn't matter how seasoned of a proposal team it is, this happens all the time.

Read the RFP.

Look for deal breakers. Make sure you have all the qualifications. Make sure it's the right fit.

And on another note, please don't wait a week to review it. Or two. RFPs never give us enough time to bid as it is, so having it sit on your desk for two weeks while the team could be working on it is just disrespectful. You're essentially saying that you don't respect people's time, and you don't respect the bottom line of your company. Ouch.

If you had a process for this, it probably wouldn't happen as frequently. Just sayin'.

We recently got a call to help with an RFP that was due in one week – ONE WEEK! This was a large federal bid, and not only was it due in one week, it had to be printed and shipped. This wasn't an electronic submittal, so you automatically lose a day.

Turns out, this RFP was released more than a month prior. The CEO of this company had it on his desk, he just hadn't looked at it. It was a green-light prospect for them so not bidding wasn't an option.

Unfortunately, that was just too short of a turnaround for my team and I to be able to make the positive impact we wanted to make, so we had to turn down the job. We knew no matter what we did, nothing was going to make a difference; the timeframe was just too short for it to be a viable contender.

When you have a strong internal process for processing RFPs that come in the door, you'll avoid situations like this.

2.8. Use Proper Grammar (Duh!)

Another "Stating the Obvious." Are you sensing a theme?

I do think it's kind of sad that I even have to include this chapter. But alas, I do.

I get that we're in a culture that doesn't use proper grammar the way that some of us old folks were taught. Times have changed. We no longer have to be so buttoned up – thank god, because I would never be writing this book if I had to be too buttoned up.

I'm not telling you that you have to be perfect. But you *will* be judged based on how easy your proposal is to read. Reality Rich may be a bit unfocused, but he notices if there are a lot of typos and poor grammar, because it makes it so much harder to read. Proper grammar leads to easier reading. Period. Reality Rich is subconsciously dinging you. No question.

The simple answer here -- use your spell & grammar check tool. That's the minimum. Don't rely on it because it isn't full-proof, but don't avoid it. It's glaringly obvious when that basic step has been skipped. You'd be surprised at how many people don't do that.

The best approach is to use the tool *and* have a separate person do an editorial proofreading. This person should be someone who hasn't been involved in the creation of the RFP, so they can come in with a clean slate. My branding coach, Ali Craig, calls it "Virgin Eyes." Get yourself a pair of those "Virgin Eyes!"

Outsource this if you need to. It's that important.

2.9. Stop The Damn Excuses

"We have a really small staff."

"Everyone is wearing multiple hats."

"They laid a bunch of people off so now I have too much work."

"The air conditioner is too cold."

"There's raisins in my chocolate chip cookie."

Yeah yeah.

We all have something going on, we are all missing something, and every single one of us could use more or less of something.

Figure out how to be creative despite the shortcomings. The most successful people and companies do this well.

When people talk to us about how we can help them be more successful in responding to RFPs, it's not just about taking their money. We ask very specific questions, such as:

- What are your immediate needs?
- What are your biggest challenges?
- What are your biggest weaknesses?
- What is your budget?

Then, we help them get the biggest bang for their buck so they are using the right resources in the right places.

Ask yourself these same questions to determine specifically what you need. Then get creative and resourceful instead of complaining about it.

"Complaining is a zero-return investment."
-Gary Vaynerchuk

THE SNAPSHOT

Key Takeaways

Mindset, strategy, and process - these build the foundation for successful RFP results. Ignore them, you'll fail. Embrace them, you'll set yourself up for winning. Sprinkle in a few other foundational elements and you'll be off to a great start.

Now, which would you rather have - failure or success?

Good answer. Now, get to work!

Resources

Throughout the book I am referencing some great resources, so make sure you take note and get what you need to do better and win more!

The RFP Success™ Kit (http://RFPSuccess.expert/kit):

- **Bidding Strategy Checklist**
- **Target Client Identifier Questions**

The RFP Success™ Institute (http://RFPSuccessInstitute.com):

- **Process Audit Checklist**

Other resources:

- www.FindRFP.com
- www.Bidnet.com

CHAPTER 3.

Stop The Insanity! The Crucial Mistakes Businesses Make When Bidding On RFPs

Let's talk about the things you need to stop immediately. These are the things that drive the buyers crazy!

If you've never watched the infamous Bob Newhart "Stop It" skit, Google it and watch the video. It's epic and falls right in suit with this section.

STOP DOING THIS

3.1. Relying On Hope

The infamous quote that I mentioned in a previous chapter, "Hope is not a strategy", hits home because it's so true.

"We really hope we win this one."

Yes, I know you hope. But your response better be based on a heck of a lot more than hope. Sadly, that's not often the case.

Tie this chapter back to the need to have a solid foundation. If you don't have all the things we discussed back in the last section "Get your *ish together", you're relying too much on hope.

You also can't rely on an outsider. My staff and I cannot make the decision to bid for you. We can ask questions, facilitate the discussion, point out pitfalls, but someone in your organization needs to own the decision and the strategy. You also understand your target clients and industry much better than we can!

Back that hope up with strategy and confidence!

STOP DOING THIS

3.2. Sitting In Frustration

Yes, RFPs can be annoying. They're contradictory, they don't make sense, many times you can't for the life of you figure out how to lay the response out because their instructions are so ambiguous. The procurement officials don't really answer your questions the way you needed them to. We could wax poetic about all the icky things that frustrate us with RFPs. All legitimate.

But here's the deal, this happens every single time. So stop being surprised by it!

The more you sit in frustration, the more you talk about the annoyances, the more you throw your hands up in the air, seemingly surprised because of the RFP, the more frustration and challenge you'll attract.

What you focus on becomes your reality. That goes double for mindset.

If you despise RFPs, you shouldn't be bidding on RFPs. Find another business development strategy. It's that simple. Or hire a team that thrives in RFP responses. But if they're always going to make you miserable, move on.

Just giving you the cold, hard truth.

STOP DOING THIS

3.3. Not Taking It Seriously

You and your entire team have to give a damn, at the highest levels of the organization because RFPs are the lifeblood of your business.

Someone in your organization needs to be the Executive Sponsor. The Executive Sponsor is the person who sets the bidding strategy, that herds the cattle, that motivates the team to pursue a particular opportunity.

If there isn't that *one person* who is really taking it seriously and sees the RFP as a solid, viable opportunity, there isn't anyone on the team who will take it seriously. It will revert to feeling like a long, arduous task.

This is a top-down conversation. If the leadership team doesn't take it seriously, don't expect the proposal team to rally and give it their best.

STOP DOING THIS

3.4. Speaking To The Written Document

Newsflash! *There is a real live human being (remember Reality Rich?!) on the other end of your RFP response.*

Crazy, right?

Of course you know this, but most people respond as if they are talking to the question or the document itself, not a real live person. It's a classic trap that we fall into because of the pages and pages of endless, process-oriented, technical questions.

When you are crafting your response, start answering as if you were talking to a live person. Picture Reality Rich. Speak it out loud if you need to. We tend to craft our answers just in response to the written question, not in response to a buyer, a human, who is reading that answer.

This will make an amazing difference in how buyers/evaluators "judge" you. They will start to see *you* as a human being as well. When you write like a human, you become more relatable. When you become more relatable, you become more likeable. And when you become more likeable- good things happen.

It doesn't matter who is on the other end of the document – no one wants to hire the wrong person/company. No one. Help them make the right decision.

STOP DOING THIS

3.5. Vomiting Expertise

Ah, one of my favorite conversations. And when I say "favorite", read: sarcasm.

There are two messages here:

First, stick to what they ask for.

You are going to be able to envision more of what the client needs than they can see for themselves. You're the expert, and you're probably ten steps ahead of where the buyer is. But you have to meet them where they are.

Resist the urge to tell them everything you know. We can get caught up in feeling the need to share everything because we think that will differentiate us, make us more appealing, and show how smart we are. Not true. You will likely overwhelm them, and an overwhelmed buyer doesn't buy.

Resist the urge to include something that is irrelevant just because you want to prove your worth.

Resist the urge to go on and on about how great you or your company is.

Resist the urge to include every report or tool in the appendix just because they are cool.

The RFP might not ask for everything you know they are going to need. You can address those things as they relate to what the RFP asks for, and you can add in some teasers, but you have to be very careful to not go overboard.

Second, the evaluators are likely not at your level.

You know those "....For Dummies" books? There are literally thousands of these books because we are all just dummies unless it's our area of expertise (I say lovingly, please don't write letters slamming me for calling you a dummy). Likely most of your evaluators are not anywhere near the level you are. We already know that Reality Rich isn't. Cut them a break, help them understand what you're saying. Think: Simple + Specific + Succinct.

Remember, YOU are the expert, not your clients. Don't assume that they know what you're talking about. You likely have to take it down a few notches to ensure that they understand what you're talking about. It might feel "dummied down" to you, too simplistic, but your reader will appreciate it.

Most magazines - even the "smart" papers or magazines - write to a 4th, 6th, or 8th grade level. Why? Because we need to consume information simply. We need the basics. Even if you're a brain surgeon, when you were first learning about the brain, you probably retained more when the concepts were explained in a simple, concise manner.

My trick? Pretend you're explaining what you do to your grandparents. That will give you a whole new perspective.

STOP DOING THIS

3.6. Putting Your Reviewers To Sleep

I've already stressed that there's a human being on the other end of the proposal. A real-life, breathing human. Someone that truly does want to get to know you.

But if you put them to sleep, they aren't going to be impressed.

Put yourself in the reviewer's shoes. Imagine that you have 3, 6, maybe even ten 100+ page RFP responses to read. Yikesahootie (as my friend Mary would say)! It's going to be pretty hard to get through those.

You want to make it interesting. If you think about it from their perspective instead of your own perspective, you can really make a difference in how you write your response.

So how can you keep them interested without boring them to tears?

- Avoid too much tech speak - if it goes over their heads and they can't understand it, they will drift off.
- Speak your customer's language. The customer doesn't always understand your language. Speak in their terms to make it easy for them to read and understand.
- Make it visually appealing - break things up so that it isn't one full page of non-stop text
- Speak in steps - describing your approach? Break it down into smaller steps (i.e., we approach this in 3 key steps: #1, #2, #3). This helps with clarity, but also breaks up the reading to keep them interested.
- Add a spark of personality!
- Tell stories

When we do proposal reviews for our clients, especially for public sector proposals, I can almost guarantee that one of our top three comments will be, "Boring!" I sure as heck don't like to be bored; but who do you know that likes to read boring? Anyone? NO! If you're reading a book and it's boring, do you keep reading? Maybe, but I guarantee you're doing your grocery list in your head.

You do *not* want your evaluators to be doing their grocery lists in their heads when they're reading your proposal. Not a great way to get them to hire you.

And think of it this way - are you writing something that you would be excited to read?

Reality Rich is hungover. He went out bowling with his buddies last night. He tried to be tame because he had to work the next day, but best laid plans. Needless to say, he's dragging, and soooo not in the mood to put much brainpower into anything. He's ready to put his head down and coast through his day.

But his boss had different plans for him.

Reality Rich's boss calls him in to a meeting to help evaluate proposals for a recent RFP that they released. He's been told to clear his schedule for the rest of the day to tackle this project. This RFP is big, and there are five bidders. Most of the responses over 100 pages. He has to read through each one and provide his scores and commentary.

Like most of us in Reality Rich's spot, the reality is, he's going to do the bare minimum. He's going to skim over the highlights and coast his day away so he can go home and go to bed. Remember, he's already unfocused to begin with, but now he's not mentally in the game at all. And he's tired.

In fact, by the time he gets to the last response, his brain is going to be mush and his energy will be gone.

How are you going to keep his attention as he reads through your response? How will you entertain Reality Rich and make him laugh? What if your response is the fifth and final response he reads? Yikes!

The truth is, we don't know what kind of a mood the evaluators are going to be in. We don't know what's going on in their day as they work through our responses. On their very best day, you need to do a great job of capturing their attention, but we certainly can't assume we'll get them all on their very best day. Knock it out of the park each time.

STOP DOING THIS

3.7. Using An Expectation As A Differentiator

A differentiator is an attribute that separates you from the rest of the companies in your space. It should be unique, measurable, and defendable.

Easily 80% of the companies that hire us can't differentiate themselves. Even those that think they know their differentiators tend to say things like, "Great customer service!", or "On-time delivery!", or "Up to date technology."

No.

Those are expectations. If I hire you, I expect you to have great customer service and on-time delivery. Have you ever had a client say, "Oh, we don't really care if you deliver when you say you're going to deliver."

No!

It's hard, I understand. Heck, I teach this and it's hard for me to do it for myself. But a differentiator sets you apart, it isn't something that is expected.

Here are a couple of examples to get your brain revved up:

Expectation:

Great customer service!

Differentiator:

99.7% 'Highly Satisfied' ratings on our customer satisfaction surveys

Expectation:

20 years' industry expertise

Differentiator:

Over the past twenty years, we have served 15 of the top 20 engineering firms in the greater Atlanta area, and have testimonials from each and every one.

Having a hard time identifying your differentiators?

Get some help!

- Ask your clients. Simply asking them why they hired you over someone else will often shed some light on what can sometimes be a difficult exercise.
- Ask your front-line employees. They often see things completely differently than people in top-level positions.
- Give us a call to help. It's what we do, and we know how to ask the right objective questions to flesh this out
- Wouldn't you know it, we've got you covered here. We have a great exercise in The RFP Success™ Institute that will walk you through this with ease.

Whatever it takes, it's important that you know your overall business differentiators, and then how you'll differentiate yourself for each individual response (it may be the same, but it may change).

When you can tap into these key attributes of your company, you will be able to demonstrate that you are the right solution for the opportunity. Without it, you're likely doomed.

If you're struggling to find your key differentiators, here are some ideas that may help:

- **Create a defined process or system** - i.e., The RFP Success™ System.
- **Quantifiable results** - 99.2% quality rating, 99.9% on-time rating, 90% 5-star ratings on Yelp (particularly if this is unique for your industry)
- **Superiority** - Best Quality (if you can really claim this and quantify it)
- **Uniqueness** - is your product or service clearly unique in any way? Meaning, you have an offering that no one else has. A trademark, a patent, a unique process or approach, etc.
- **Simplicity or efficiency** - do you provide a simple or efficient way to do things that your competitors don't?
- **Market dominance** -#1 or #2 in an industry category
- **Guarantee** - if you have a unique type of guarantee, or if having a guarantee is unique in your industry
- **First-to-market** - were you the "first" to do something a certain way? Did you start the trend? Claim that!
- **Awards**

No matter what differentiator or combination of differentiators you choose, you want to make sure you stand out!

STOP DOING THIS

3.8. Ignoring Your Competition

One of the beautiful things about public sector bidding is that you can often get copies of the winning and/or competitor bids. If you don't do this now, implement this practice immediately!

In private sector bidding, it might not be as easy as getting copies of your competitors' proposals, but you still need to know your key competitors.

Knowing not only *who* your competitors are, but what their strengths and weaknesses are, is a no-brainer.

You should know……

- Who the key players are in your space
- What their strengths and weaknesses are
- Who their clients are
- Who is the low-baller
- Who are the up-and-comers
- How do they differentiate themselves

Creating a competitor profile for your top three to five competitors and monitoring them on a regular basis will give you a huge advantage.

This requires a process (big surprise!). Having competitor profiles, knowing how to find the information, and tracking recent events and news should be part of that process.

We have a research team that provides this service for our clients. We created a standard profile and video training so that no matter who on that research team is conducting the research, they know what we are looking for and the best way to go about it. That process has benefitted us greatly. See, create the process!

If you want to see this in action, check out our RFP Success™ Institute for a full training and the profile we use for our clients.

STOP DOING THIS

3.9. Wasting Time

You waste time when you don't have a strategy. Because when you don't have a strategy, you bid on things you shouldn't be bidding on.

You waste time when you don't have a process. Because when you don't have a process, you'll miss things, you won't anticipate appropriately, and you'll have to back track too much.

Do you think I've beaten that dead horse enough?

Wasting time isn't a luxury we generally have when we're bidding on RFPs because we are working on tight deadlines. And even if you are super organized, even if you have great processes and strategies, there WILL still be challenges. That will all make it easier and quicker to overcome, but challenges will still arise. It's the nature of the beast.

STOP DOING THIS

3.10. Doing It All Yourself

This chapter goes out to all the small business owners who are trying to do this on their own.

Hear this: You can't.

You can't possibly respond to RFPs as a single person. Well, you can, but you won't be very successful. And you'll burn yourself out in the meantime.

When you try to do it yourself, you miss out on things like:

- Objectivity
- Details
- Checks and balances

I get that not every company can afford to hire a robust proposal team. Hey, that's why my company is in business, because we supplement where companies can't afford or don't need full-time staff.

If you can't afford to get outside help, get creative with it. And think about what the best use of your time is. The higher up the food chain you are, the better your time is spent on the high yield activities (meaning: making money!).

Here are some creative things that I've seen small companies do, or we've recommended to our clients:

- Hire interns. They are generally eager to learn your industry and are much less expensive than bringing in an experienced person. The down side? You're going to have to spend some time training.

- Outsource specific items of the proposal – you can hire a Virtual Assistant to format or proofread your proposal if you don't have an internal assistant to do that; you can hire an inexpensive graphic designer to help add some graphical elements
- If you have a business colleague or friend who is in the same boat as you are, trade proposal review tasks ("I'll review yours if you'll review mine" approach)

Looking for more inspiration on how to get support on your budget?

I got ya!

Checkout The RFP Success™ Kit for free templates and checklists (http://RFPSuccess.expert/kit), The RFP Success™ Institute for complete learning modules and community (http://RFPSuccessInstitute.com), or connect with our RFP Success™ Community on LinkedIn.

❑ Don't Just Take My Word For It...

Meet Talmar Anderson. Talmar is ah-mazing at that thing many of us don't love – hiring and managing. She is the voice of reason – in a very direct yet passionate way – so we can get out of our own way and get the right help at the right time. And she does it with a bourbon in hand. Who doesn't love that?!

***

Employee or Contractors – Who Does the Work?

When a small business is looking to design the workforce on a project, a common sticking point is whether to bring on employees or outsource pieces to independent contractors. There is a definite time and place for each of these and it will be specific to 3 things:

Your growth,

Your budget and

(most importantly) the business' need!

*If you are trending up in your revenues – then yes hire employees NOW! This is a definite "yes" if your company is bidding on, and winning several RFPs, and your business development department needs the support. Not only will you be hiring to beef up your RFP production team, you will be hiring for your deliverable fulfillment and operational structures. Don't just stand around...**go get busy with your hiring process!***

What if you need specialized expertise that you don't have in-house? Or perhaps you have someone in-house that can handle the financial projects, the graphics and formatting of the layout but you need a great RFP writer or objective reviewer? Maybe your company does not dedicate energy to cultivate RFP awards but are happy to bid on them when they pop up? In this case, your budget does not justify an employee that will work with you 52 weeks a year.

Does this only happen a few times a year or not even consistently? This is a great time to bring on a strong independent contractor. Somebody that your company could work with repeatedly so that all that time they get to know you, and your business can be compounded and reused. By the second or third time, the specifics and data collection process will be streamlined and may even save you some money!

The risk, of course, is that they may not always be available when you call them up. Great independent contractors can get booked up. That risk is far outweighed by the knowledge that you do not have to carry the full year payroll (and benefits!) of an employee that will likely have spots throughout the year that they cannot contribute to your company's success.

When should you outsource all or part of your RFP, or any process, to a sub-contractor or consultant?

A quick guide is if your company:

- *Requires the support of 20 or less hours a month (more than that requires, in most states, you hiring them as an employee);*
- *Is NOT interested in learning about or managing the specific piece because your company will not need to deliver on it with any consistency;*
- *Values expert insight – Short deadlines or high insider requirements can lead to outsourcing to deliver a more polished, on point and oftentimes faster product.*

The hiring and management of subs and consultants can be as time intensive as an employee while on project. Until your business requires more time invested to produce more work than that it is usually in your company's best interest to work with a professional in that specific pace.

*The good news? Contracting is great because the company you hire to work with **LITERALLY DOES IT** for a living. They must be experts, current on concepts and experienced at the results you are looking for on this project. (And you know all of this because you ARE checking their references like an employee, right?! I know I am bossy. I get that a lot!). Many companies are structured to take on more clients so you do not have to worry about lack of availability to support your deadlines. If you are not in the business of say, RFP writing, then a subcontractor/consultant can get it done. That is one less thing that your company needs to focus upon.*

*She's bossy because she knows her *ish, so heed her advice!*

This is the fun of having a kickass team around you. Everyone (employees, independent contractors and vendors) will all work with your business, getting things done (sometimes better than you!) to get you closer to that success, those goals and those opportunities you are looking for within your business! Now GO! Grow!

Talmar Anderson,
Hiring & Management Expert
Boss Actions

***

Thanks, Talmar! Seriously great input because I know a lot of businesses struggle with "when is the right time?" You're a woman after my own heart with the simple approach.

STOP DOING THIS

3.11. Putting The Wrong People In The Wrong Roles

Let's be honest, you're actually probably going to do this if you're a small company. In those instances, it's all hands on deck. But you need to be very cognizant of what you're doing and have a game plan to transition away from this approach as you can afford additional help.

If you're a larger company without dedicated writers, you probably fall into the trap of having the writers be anyone who is available. Also the wrong answer. By doing this, you're not putting your best foot forward.

Start by defining what it is you need in your response team members. Then make sure you are filling those roles with the best available resources. Put your best foot forward, otherwise why even bother?

In the early days of one of my prior employers, we were a small shop. We had limited resources, and it was often an "all-hands-on-deck" approach to responding to RFPs.

The way we handled who would be part of the response team was whoever was available. Great strategy, right? And guess who was generally available? The 'C' players. Not the 'A' or 'B' players, but the ones that didn't have enough work because they weren't the most sought-after team members.

There we were, putting the least qualified people to work on one of the most important business activities – selling!

It took some time for us to shift our mindset, and then figure out how to get the right people involved with the right opportunities. Eventually, it became second nature.

STOP DOING THIS

3.12. Making Assumptions

Ack! We make so many assumptions when responding to RFPs, most of which are subconscious. Things like....

- We assume they know as much as we do - you might have one person in the room that is deeply familiar with your industry. Most others on the evaluation committee (ahem – Reality Rich) probably have knowledge of one little piece of the puzzle, if that. Assume that the reviewers don't know what you know, and then speak plain language. Don't confuse them and don't tech speak. Make it simple for them to understand.

- We assume the Reality Riches of the world have all the time in the world to read our proposals. Um, no. They are busy, they're juggling a ton of stuff. This is one more task added to their already full plate. They're probably annoyed going into it. Not a great way to start. That's why you've got to capture their attention and keep them interested.

- We assume that because they wrote the RFP, the sequence will feel logical to them – it's likely that the people on the evaluation committee didn't have any involvement in putting together the RFP, so it may make no more logical sense to them than it does to you. Even the person who created the RFP likely pulled several pieces together to make up the whole and they don't even know what they did.

- We assume that they know the ins and outs of the entire RFP – not all members of the evaluation committee care about the entirety of the RFP. Many of them may have a stake in just a small portion of the project. Because of this, they are likely to focus solely on the portion that is relevant to them. Make sure the sections can stand alone and don't continuously reference other sections.

- We assume that the information is going to be interesting to all reviewers - think about it, in some instances they are reviewing upwards of ten proposals. That's a LOT of reading. Even three proposals is a lot to review. Keep the reading simple, interesting, and easy to follow and the reviewers will appreciate you!

There's so many assumptions but these are the top five that we see on a regular basis. Best to rid yourself of these assumptions.

STOP DOING THIS

3.13. Acting Like You Need Them More Than They Need You

Please stop reeking of desperation. It stinks!

"We have to win!"

We put so much pressure on ourselves to constantly win that we reek of desperation. If you are feeling that way, it's going to affect your confidence. And when you aren't confident, it's going to show in your response.

It's a common misconception, but you do not need them more than they need you. We are looking for a win-win proposition. We want to find the right opportunity that suits our businesses while providing the best solution to our clients.

I hate to say it yet again (oh, who am I kidding, I *love* saying it!), but it comes down to having a strategy. And differentiators. Having those will boost your confidence so you're not approaching it from a place of fear or desperation.

It's really that simple.

STOP DOING THIS

3.14. Competing On Price Alone

Unless you are claiming the space of low-cost leader, stop competing on price alone!

Walmart does it because that is their value proposition. But it's probably not yours.

Is one of your differentiators low cost? If so, then own that and shout it from the rooftops!

Otherwise, the only time you should be competing on price alone is if you are trying to "buy the business" to get into a new market or industry.

Everyone thinks it's about price. That's becoming less and less the case. Very rarely do we see price account for more than 20-30% anymore, if that. Buyers are getting much savvier because they have gotten burned by hiring based mostly on price.

Haven't you? Think of a time when you decided to go the least expensive way and it hasn't gone well. I guarantee you that you won't do that again for that particular product or service.

Clients want value. They want good value for the money they are going to spend. They don't want to just throw money away, but value is becoming much more important.

Value comes in all shapes and sizes – productivity, effectiveness, efficiencies, proprietary tools, etc. How does your company add value that goes beyond price?

We go deeper into the topic of Value on page 144, so make sure you don't skip over that!

The other question you have to ask yourself is this: If a particular client cares only about low-cost provider, why would you bid?

THE SNAPSHOT

Key Takeaways

You can't be boring. Period.

Not only can you not be boring, but you've got to find a way to stand out, to differentiate yourself.

And you've got to take it seriously; you and everyone at all levels of your organization.

Chapter 4.

Do More Of This To Get Bigger And Better Results

All right, let's focus now on what you should be doing. There are so many great things you can do to stand out from the competition and make the buyers take notice.

That's what it's all about, after all!

DO MORE OF THIS

4.1. Quantify

We humans love statistics.

Facts and figures make us feel smart. They give us something to sink our teeth into. We will remember something much longer and easier when it's quantifiable, even if we don't remember the exact number.

The more you can quantify things, the better.

Clients love nothing more than to see actual results that they can relate to.

Add more quantifiable data to your proposals. Reality Rich can really hang his hat on the number of clients that you have in the same industry, or the percentage of on-time deliveries that you have. Don't be dry and boring about it, you can put it into a chart, add it to a call-out, make it pop so Reality Rich really notices it. And remember, simplicity is still key here.

What should you be quantifying?

- Customer satisfaction information
- Quality ratings
- On-time %'s
- Growth

Anything that speaks to the outcome that you will provide to your clients is great when you can put a number to it.

DO MORE OF THIS

4.2. Be Conscious

It's no surprise that I love a well-oiled proposal process and team. Nothing makes me happier than when I meet a team that has it all together. They love their jobs, they have great strategies and processes, they do a great job of vetting opportunities and they win a lot.

What's the one thing they have in common?

They can fall into the trap of the unconscious.

It happens to ALL of us.

> *When I started drafting this book I sent a couple of chapters to my editor. She came back and basically said it was crap (okay fine, she was much nicer than that). What she said was, I wasn't practicing what I was preaching. I was writing this buttoned up, straight-laced professional book that no doubt was full of great strategies, but it wasn't fun. It didn't have any personality. It was heavy. It was b-o-r-i-n-g.*
>
> *Ouch!*
>
> *I think my biggest fear in life is being boring.*
>
> *But she was spot on. I got back in touch with the ultimate outcome that I wanted for this book, which is to provide tips and strategies in a fun, efficient, and simple way to help businesses create more RFP Success™! Once I got conscious, I was back on track.*

Sometimes we are not conscious to what we are doing – in other words, we are on autopilot.

We are juggling too many things. We are going through the motions to get something done, but we aren't conscious to the desired outcome.

Step back and ask yourself, what are you trying to accomplish? What is the ultimate message (aka your Proposal Promise), and how are you addressing that?

DO MORE OF THIS

4.3. COMMUNICATE

It never ceases to amaze me at how awful so many people in leadership positions are at communicating. Not necessarily because they are bad at the communication itself, but because they avoid it. So many people would rather assume or avoid than meet it head on.

It's no different in the world of RFPs. Of course, the whole premise of an RFP is communicating your message and your answers to the RFP questions in written format.

But you should also be communicating when……

You decline to bid. If this is a green light target for you, or even a yellow light target, you'll want to communicate that you are declining to bid and why. If you are declining to bid because something isn't right with the proposal, your client may thank you. It also gives you an opportunity to get your name in front of the prospect. Always take advantage of this opportunity. Someone like Reality Rich is really going to remember this.

You need clarity. There is generally a bidder's conference or Q&A period where you can ask questions. Ask your questions. Stop avoiding the question because you're afraid that it's going to give something away to your competitors. Ask smart questions to get what you need in order to provide the best solution.

A colleague was recently telling me a story about her consulting firm bidding on a proposal for a large retailer. They were wildly confused by the scope of work (we've never seen that happen, have we??!). There was a virtual bidder's conference and they decided to ask some very pointed questions to better understand what they were bidding on.

One of the questions they asked the client was, "What is your expected outcome for this project?"

Can you believe, the client didn't really have the answer? After some additional questions and quite a bit of discussion, the client themselves gained clarity around what they were ultimately trying to accomplish. This changed the approach for how my colleague's company responded.

Now, because this question was asked in a public forum, this also allowed their competitors to change their approach. However, the client recognized that the approach my colleague's firm took at that bidder's conference was the type of approach they wanted in their partner for this project, and they won the work.

You can't be afraid to ask the tough questions and communicate when something doesn't look quite right. If the client doesn't appreciate that, they probably aren't the right client for you.

Remember, you're not desperate.

DO MORE OF THIS

4.4. Anticipate & Troubleshoot

Strategy, Process. Mindset. They can all be seemingly top notch, and things will still go wrong. It's just the way things go. Weather happens. Technology happens. Humans happen.

The more prepared you are to troubleshoot, the better off you are.

Be the MacGyver of RFP responses!

(if you're too young to understand that reference, look it up. Or read: resourceful).

Anticipate: **Slipped deadlines.** First thing to remember is that it ALWAYS takes longer to finalize the proposal than you think. Anticipate that.

Anticipate: **Changes.** Don't forget to allow time for updating after someone has reviewed. There will always be changes for each person that reviews it.

Troubleshoot: **What do you do when production is behind and may not finish in time?** Get on the phone and find a local printer who can print/produce half of the proposals. This takes the pressure off of one production facility having to handle it all. Know all of your shipping options. If production isn't going to be on time, that delays delivery. For proposals that have a hard date and time deadline, you can't mess around here. Know all of your production and shipping options. Research your options way ahead of time and get creative!

TROUBLESHOOT: A key team member is out sick. In your planning, you should always have a back-up identified for each of the key roles. This will help prevent panic if a team member is out sick and unable to fulfill their responsibilities.

TROUBLESHOOT: You're running out of time to finish the proposal. The best thing to do in this situation is to pay attention to the scoring criteria. Make sure you hit on their top challenges, and make sure you meet the proposal requirements. Some other areas can take a back seat to that. Of course, if you're too far behind and you'll be submitting a sub-par proposal, you may need to pull the plug, but that's never the ideal situation.

My team and I were recently working with a client on a very large RFP. They have a great internal process and team who is a well-oiled machine. We got down to crunch time and were doing the final review when we realized that the two reviewers were reviewing from two completely different documents.

What happened is that the RFP itself was a Word document and parts of it somehow got changed (read: things got inadvertently erased), so one reviewer didn't have a complete document.

It set us back a few hours but we were able to pull it out. But if we hadn't realized this, that could have resulted in submitting an incorrect response and possibly being disqualified.

DO MORE OF THIS

4.5. Tier Your Answers

The people reviewing your RFP response are at all different levels of knowledge, different levels of interest, different positions in the organization. Frankly, you can't even guarantee that they are going to read everything you write.

That's why we recommend having a tiered approach to answering each question where applicable.

Tier One: It's very simple - right up front, make one simple and succinct statement that addresses the question they have asked. Generally, you can do this in one sentence. If they ask a yes/no question, literally answer the question with a yes or a no, and then repeat back the question in answer format. Reality Rich is a Tier One reader, that's probably all you're going to get out of him. Make it worthwhile.
Tier Two: If possible, break out the steps at a high level that address their question. Make this a list of steps versus a long paragraph.
Tier Three: This is where you can go into much more detail.

This approach allows the different levels of interest and understanding to get what they need.

Those that are going to skim will likely only read the first tier. Great, they will know that you meet the qualifications and they may even keep reading to your second tier.

Those that need more detail will get what they need with your second and third tier.

You make everyone happy and you meet them where they are. Well done!

DO MORE OF THIS

4.6. Dummy It Down

Here we are again with that word "Dummy." If you don't like that word, don't fret. Think of in terms of simplicity.

Most well-known magazines and newspapers write to no more than an 8th grade level. They do this for two reasons:

1. They want to relate to a broad audience;
2. They know we need to consume information in a simple manner.

You want to speak in terms that anyone can understand. It's the grandma test that I mentioned earlier. If you had to describe it to your grandma, how would you do that?

Write to various levels of understanding in your proposal. There are likely varying levels of experience and expertise in the people who are reading your proposal.

It takes a lot of constraint to write simply while still getting your message across. And when we are the experts, we are many levels above that simplicity.

Here's a formula to keep in mind as you write:

Simple + Specific + Succinct

Keep the concepts simple. Be specific in what you are describing. But also keep it succinct so you don't lose your readers. That may feel a bit contradictory, but it's a checks and balances. You'll need to balance the desire to get into the granular details with keeping it simple and succinct.

One of my most favorite things my team and I offer is that we do proposal reviews, and these reviews span all sorts of industries. We aren't likely going to have an intimate knowledge of the industry for the review that we're are doing. Yet, when we can pick up a proposal and get a good understanding of how they will approach the project, it's already a winner. Sadly, that rarely happens. Most often we have to read it six times in order to fully grasp the concept. Much too complicated.

To help you begin to master this, check out the **Checks and Balances Checklist** in The RFP Success™ Kit (http://RFPSuccess.expert/kit). Use the Checks and Balances Checklist before you submit each and EVERY RFP.

Reality Rich just purchased some bookshelves for his new home office. They were the do-it-yourself assembly type. He pulled out the instructions and got to work putting them together.

He quickly came into a challenge – the instructions weren't making any sense. They were wildly confusing to an unfocused Reality Rich, and the parts didn't seem to match up. Frankly, there were so many parts that he just threw them all into a pile and had no interest in sorting through them. He immediately got frustrated and wanted to give up.

But then……

He decided to check on YouTube and found Bob. Bob created a video on how to assemble these exact same bookshelves. Bob was a likeable guy and extremely straightforward and succinct in his instructions. One step at a time, he verbally explained and visually demonstrated the assembly. Not only that, Bob was quite entertaining, cracking jokes and whistling quippy tunes throughout his video.

He had Reality Rich at "Hello."

Okay, so the bookshelves are not an RFP, but this is a glimpse into the mind of Reality Rich. He isn't someone who is going to take the time to learn the complex; he needs to not only have things be simple, but he wants to be entertained.

Learn from Bob. Be Bob.

DO MORE OF THIS

4.7. Follow Up

I hate to use the old saying, but it's so true that I have to go there – the fortune is in the follow-up.

It doesn't matter if you win, lose, or decline to bid – following up after the final contract is awarded will set you up for future success. Yup, it should be part of your strategy and your process (funny how those keep popping up, eh?).

Here are some key things you need to do as a follow up:

Get copies of the scoring sheets. This is more relevant to public sector proposals, but you want to request copies of the final scoring sheets, win or lose. This gives you valuable information on which areas of your proposal scored well, and which didn't.

Get copies of your competitor proposals and a copy of the final contract. Again, this is relevant to public sector proposals because that's when this type of information is available. Don't be shy, ask. You may get a no every now and then, but a lot of this is available under the Freedom of Information Act – that's why you'll sometimes hear people say, submit a FOIA (pronounced foy-yuh) request.

Request a debrief. Public or private sector, you want to ask for a debrief to get as much insight as you can into why you lost. Reality Rich loves to hop on the phone with vendors because he knows it will help him get better proposals in the future. Prepare in advance with some very specific questions. You should always lead this debrief meeting, not the client.

Even if you won..... Even if you win, you still want to ask the question, "What made you choose us?" Generally, we lose sight of this because we don't care. We have the business, the client chose us. We assume we submitted a fantastic proposal and that's why we won. Not always. Ask the question.

Send a thank you note. Win or lose (yes, either way!), send a thank you note; a hand-written, personal thank you note to the main buyer, addressing the entire team. You won't believe the kind of impact this will make.

The number of people that never follow up after a proposal is mind-boggling. This step alone will set you apart from the rest.

Follow up to get the information you need to be your badass strategic self, and to keep the lines of communication going with the buyer for continuous relationship-building.

The work should never end if this is a green-light (or even yellow-light) client. Be prepared way in advance for that next proposal.

DO MORE OF THIS

4.8. Apply The "So What?" Test

I'm going to ask you to stretch a little bit here. This requires some time and discipline to make this work. And I know what you're thinking – that you never have enough time. But guess what? You can train yourself to have more time. More often than not, it's just a matter of re-training yourself to add this step.

When you write something, it may feel relevant to you, but it isn't always the right thing to include. There has to be a reason to include it other than just your desire to share that information.

This is where the "So What?" principle comes in.

When you start to add something that goes beyond the specific question asked in the RFP, you need to ask yourself one question:

"So What?"

If you can answer that question of yourself with a response that adds value to what you're saying, by all means include that information. If you can't, leave it out.

You'll likely find that a high percentage of what you have the urge to include won't pass this test. It will force you to approach your response in a fresh light.

Asking yourself this question throughout the response ensures that you aren't including irrelevant information.

Say something worthwhile
or don't say it at all.

DO MORE OF THIS

4.9. Track Your Numbers

How do you know how many people hours it's going to take you to respond to an RFP?

How do you know what chance you have to win?

How do you know how much money you spend on each RFP response?

Eh, so you don't know the answers to these questions. So What?! (see, you're already learning to take my advice from the previous chapter! {queue applause}).

Here's why the answers to those questions are so important:

1. When it's time to hire staff to help you, how will you know what you need?
2. If you want to get extra help (a-hem, engage us!), how will you know what your budget is?
3. How will you know, other than trying to remember in your head, if you have a winning or losing track record?
4. How will you know if the cost of bidding is worth that contract price? You don't want to spend $10k to bid on a $50k project.

You've gotta track the numbers.
You can't manage if you don't measure.
And if you don't manage, well,
things are going to be bad.

Bad?! What do you mean by bad, Lisa?

- You'll bid on things that cost you more to bid than the contract value. That sucks! Because you will LOSE money. Not an option.
- You'll never be able to hire outside help because you won't know the value. That's okay, keep spinning your wheels and getting more and more exhausted, I'm sure you don't mind (tongue in cheek).
- You'll never be ready to hire the right kind of staff to help you build on your bidding strategy and keep you winning more business. And if you're not moving forward, why are you in business (a little cold harsh truth there)?

So, what should you track? Here are some essentials:

- Track what you bid on
- Track what you win.
- Track what you lose.
- Track what you decline.
- Track how much time/money/resources it takes you to respond.
- Track which competitors win and lose.

Love the idea of tracking and managing, but a bit lost on exactly "How?" I totally understand. And like always I've got you with a sample tracking sheet in the RFP Success™ Kit. We even go into a deeper dive training in The RFP Success™ Institute. So don't worry, we've got this!

This should all be part of your strategy & process (!!!) and will help guide you to make good decisions about bidding, hiring, and outsourcing, and set you up for when the contract is coming to a close for potential future opportunities.

Create your ideal system to keep track of all this information. You can use a simple Excel spreadsheet like we share in The RFP Success™ Kit (http://RFPSuccess.expert/kit), or find a fancy tracking software. Find something that works best for your environment and team.

Data is King. And Queen. And the Royal Court.

Consider this very simplistic example....

Let's say it costs you $10,000 to respond to each RFP and you respond to two RFPs a month. Average contract value is $500k.

At a 20% win rate, your cost to bid is 10% of total contract value.

At a 50% win rate, your cost to bid is only 4% of total contract value.

So What?

Not only is a higher win rate better because you get more business, but your cost to bid will actually go down. That leaves the door open to hire more help.

Could you use more help? I'd be shocked if the answer was no.

Know your numbers!

DO MORE OF THIS

4.10. Create An Opportunity Scorecard

Let's circle back to process and strategy (insert big cheesy grin here).

An Opportunity Scorecard helps you assess each individual opportunity against pre-determined criteria. Some people call this go/no go, some call it bid/no bid. I like Opportunity Scorecard. If you don't have an Opportunity Scorecard, you won't have any criteria for making a decision on what to bid on.

If you don't have criteria for making a decision on what to bid on, you'll bid on everything that looks decent. And you'll make a lot of bad decisions.

When you make bad decisions on what to bid on, you waste time, money and resources. You burn out yourself and your staff. You lose a lot.

Creating an Opportunity Scorecard not only makes the decision process easier, but it allows you to train other people on your team in this process so you don't have to do it all yourself. Wouldn't that be nice?!

Here's what you should include in your Opportunity Scorecard (and oh, by the way, there's an **Opportunity Scorecard Checklist** in The RFP Success™ Kit):

Create a list of must-haves. Create a list of 8-10 things that are must-haves in order to bid on the business. These are things like: Is it the right kind of client; do you have enough time to bid; do you have enough staff to do the work, do you have an existing relationship; is there alignment with the company goals and strategy.

Know what you're willing to accept in legal terms. These bids generally have large and complex terms and conditions. What are you willing to sign off on?

Know what your deal breakers are. Are you a company that will never bid if cost accounts for more than 50% of the scoring? Are there on-site requirements that you can't accommodate? What about insurance or performance bond requirements? Know what your deal breakers are.

Know where you're willing to compromise. You should know up front what your company is and isn't willing to compromise on. When you identify this information as part of your overall strategy, you won't be fumbling around in the middle of a proposal.

I have actually dedicated one chapter to reading the damn proposal right when you get it. This is why. Because you need to be aware of what might stop you in your tracks.

Back in my consulting days, we bid on pretty much anything that came in the door for our specialty practice. We were the leaders in our space and there seemed to be no reason not to bid.

As we got much more strategic, it became clear that we shouldn't be bidding on everything. We created a list of criteria and turned it into an actual scoring tool – an Excel spreadsheet with formulas that spit out an actual score that we could use to assess each opportunity (hey, I worked with an office full of accountants and actuaries – Excel was a way of life and they loved stuff like this!). And before you ask, "Yes" we have a resource in the RFP Success™ Kit waiting for you – http://RFPSuccess.expert/kit.

What became great about this was that we could get staff at all levels involved in this process. All they had to do was answer a handful of yes/no questions. Based on their answers, the tool would create a score for them. Then they would take that information to the Client Manager. This prevented the Client Manager from having to read all RFPs that crossed their desk, therefore saving a ton of time. It helped our younger staff understand how we made business development decisions, so when we did decide to bid on something, they were committed because they understood why.

Win-win!

You don't have to be so fancy, but find something that works for you and stick with it each and every time.

DO MORE OF THIS

4.11. Walk Away If It Isn't Right

Lisa, are you crazy?!

Remember when I told you to stop bidding out of desperation and fear? That person will never walk away. They will bid on everything because they *need* it. And they certainly won't pull the plug halfway through the response.

When you are bidding strategically, you'll know when to go all in, and when to pull the plug. When you have your **Opportunity Scorecard** in place, you'll be able to assess appropriately. And you'll start to "feel" when something isn't right. And when it isn't right, you don't want to force it.

If it's too hard at the bidding stage (we're talking working with the prospect here, not the process of responding), it's probably going to be hard throughout the entire engagement. If the client is difficult now, imagine what they'll be like two or three years into a five-year contract?

In my early consulting days, we were that desperate client. We bid on anything and everything because we felt like we had to. We were in growth mode, and we wanted all the clients we could get.

I very specifically remember working on a bid that threw up hurdle after hurdle. The requirements of the RFP were incredibly unclear, leading us to believe they didn't know what they wanted. They were very short and tight-lipped in responding to our questions. Most of their responses led us to believe that they didn't foster an environment of open communication but assumed we would know the answers to everything.

We ended up winning the 3-year contract for employee benefits consulting. And they were a nightmare client. We should have walked away when we were feeling that they didn't value partnerships. They didn't want to answer questions, and that followed through in our work with them. They were hard to communicate with, leading us to have to make a lot of assumptions that were not always right.

We couldn't wait to get rid of that client.

Not every client is the right client. Learn to walk away.

DO MORE OF THIS

4.12. Make It Easy On The Reviewers

Remember hungover Reality Rich? He needed to have an easy day. He needed the respondents to make it easy on him because he was having a tough day.

The easier you can make things on your reviewers, the more they will appreciate you. They might not even realize it in the moment, but they appreciate it.

We always need to keep in mind that the reviewers are likely evaluating multiple proposals. The responses get boring, tedious, and -- let's face it -- flat out annoying. Keeping this in mind, it's imperative that we "make friends" with our reviewers very early on in our response.

Tell the reviewers what they need to know up front. You want to demonstrate right out of the gate that you have met all of their requirements. Obviously (and hopefully!) you've done that throughout your response, but you want them to know that on Page 1 when they are forming their initial impression, not on page 100 when they're paying less attention. This is the time to inject some subconscious persuasion that will stick in the evaluator's mind for the rest of the response.

Have you ever heard the phrase, "above the fold"? That references the upper half of the front page of a newspaper. Most papers are folded in half so that only the top half of the front page is visible at first glance. These newspapers (yeah yeah, a dying breed!) are very strategic about what they put "above the fold" because it might be the only thing someone reads. Same concept.

Here are some things you can do to make things easier on the reviewers:

Include a compliance grid. Create a table grid that outlines their high-level requirements and how you complied with each requirement. Include a page or section number for easy reference. We go so far as to include a checkmark, because it's a visual representation that a specific requirement is complete.

Include the actual RFP question in your response. If you don't include the question that the RFP asks and only include your answer, you are presuming that the reviewers remember the questions. They don't. No matter how much knowledge they have of the RFP, they won't remember. That will cause them to have to go back to the RFP itself and continue to cross-reference to a whole other document. That's just too much work. Unless there is a strict page number requirement, always include their question in your response. Don't assume that they have intimate knowledge of the RFP. They don't.

Include the yes or no. If they ask a yes/no question, answer it with a yes or no. Psychologically, you want them to automatically know that yes, you do indeed meet that criteria. Then follow up with the detail.

Use their verbiage. Repeat their question in your answer, at least as the first part of your question. That ensures you are using their language, which likely resonates with them more than any fancy schmancy language you might use.

> *Example:*
>
> Q: Can you provide drug screening either on-site or within a five-mile radius of our main office?
> A: Yes, we can provide drug screening both on-site and within a five-mile radius of your main office.

The other thing this does is ensure that you are actually answering the question as they have asked it. More on that in a little while.

Don't reference another section in your answer without also giving them the reference point and something to sink their teeth into. For example, if you're going to reference "a prior section", give them the specific section number, or a page number, and then give them a little bit of context. Don't just say something like, "We have included the answer in a prior section".

Also, be limited with how much you do this. If you constantly have them flipping back and forth, they'll get annoyed. You're making it too hard on them.

BUT, don't make it easy for them to disqualify you. Making a bad impression out of the gate is not cool. First impressions matter, so pay attention.

Reality Rich is in charge of an RFP that was released for HR Consulting Services. Today's the due date, and as with all public sector RFPs there's a definitive location and time that the RFPs have to be delivered. This is always interesting for Reality Rich, because inevitably someone has a heart-breaking story about how their dog ate their homework which caused them to be late. Sorry, but Reality Rich just can't care.

Sure enough, six bids come in by the deadline, but he knows there were seven companies who submitted Letters of Intent to Bid. Wonder what happened to the seventh?

Reality Rich logs the bids that arrived on time, checks the proposals to make sure each company has submitted the right number of copies, and distributes them to the evaluation team. Over the next few days, the evaluation team will work on reviewing each of the six bids.

The next day, Reality Rich receives a box of binders (aka responses) from the seventh company. He can see that they shipped them overnight two days ago, but the carrier just delivered them. One day late. Unfortunately, Reality Rich has the unpleasant task of contacting the bidder to let them know they are disqualified. The bidder begs and pleads, but there's nothing Reality Rich can do. They missed the deadline, they're out.

Here are some of Reality Rich's immediate observations on the rest of the bids:

- *Four of the bids are presented in 3-ring binders; one is spiral-bound; and one is held together with a binder clip. Annoying! Who is this wildly unprofessional company that just gave us a binder clip? He takes a glance at the company name. Ugh! He moves it to the bottom of the pile.*

- *One of the 3-ring binders is extra-large in comparison to the others. He immediately thumbs through it to see what the difference was, and it appears that the Appendix is full of brochures and extraneous information that isn't necessarily relevant. He rolls his eyes and chuckles. To the bottom of the pile it goes.*

- *He briefly glances over the other four bids — and he notices a company name that he recognizes, but it's a distant recognition. He can't quite put his finger on who this company is. A few minutes later he remembers. He met this guy at a networking event! He opens his desk drawer to look at the pile of business cards he has, and finds the guy — and then he notices that he wrote the word, "tool" on his card. That's Reality Rich's term for "I don't really like this guy." Hmm. He immediately thinks he's not too excited to read that bid. To the bottom of the pile it goes.*

Reality Rich now has three bids that he's going to put his focus and attention on. Just like that, he's got a poor impression of three bids. If you're one of the first three, you better hope (and remember, hope is NOT a strategy) that the other evaluators put more stock in your bid (not likely). If you're one of the three that he's going to focus on, you're in much better shape. But now, you've got to keep his attention and make an impression.

Are you confident?

DO MORE OF THIS

4.13. Set The Response Team Up For Success

A lot of times there are multiple people within a responding organization providing input for the response. Unless only one person is handling the entire response (which, remember, I don't recommend), there is room for interpretation because we all see things differently.

Here are some of our best practices when we are managing a response for a client, when they have a cross-section of client team members providing input on the response:

Create a table or template. Create a specific format for how you want them to respond. Let's say that the RFP is requiring a summary of each key personnel's experience, background and references. Instead of just telling each team member to address that question (which leaves huge room for error!), create a table that they can use to respond into.

This table should lay it out with exact questions you want them to answer.

Here's an example from a recent RFP:

> *Information required should include: timeframe, company name, company location, position title held during the term of the contract/project and details of contract/project.*

Because there were multiple asks within just this one statement, if we had asked the team to provide this information based on this statement alone, there would have been a lot missing. Instead, we provided a table that included each of these line items, so it would be hard to skip any part of the questions.

If a question has multiple parts to it, you may want to create some sort of table or template for each part of the question to make sure the writers address each part of the question.

Share the proposal promise. A proposal promise is basically a theme that you will weave throughout your proposal that you want your reviewers to really sink their teeth into. We'll delve deeper into this coming up on page 122. The more the respondents understand what the overall promise is, the better they can write to that promise.

Tell them exactly what you need from them. Don't just share the RFP with the contributors and tell them to create an answer without giving them any direction or guidelines. You may want to give them a general idea of length of their response. Maybe you want them to break things out into process steps. Tell them exactly what you want, as much as you know at the onset of the response. The other thing is, most team members aren't going to read the whole RFP. You're going to have to spell it out for them.

When you do this upfront, you prevent a ton of back-and-forth aggravation. That back-and-forth takes time, and no one has extra time. This is a great way to get some time back!

❑ Don't Just Take My Word For It...

Remember our hiring expert, Talmar Anderson (pg.72) She's got some great advice when it comes to telling people what you want, and I was able to boss her into sharing with us yet again. See how I did that??

***

When I hear stories of bosses that start with "I TOLD them that I wanted it green! Who doesn't understand green?", I take a deep breath and sigh. I know that poor company is suffering for sure! I can see the delays. I can imagine the expense of duplicating efforts. I can feel everyone's shoulders rising and knotting up with dissatisfaction. Let me make it a little clearer for you, the reader.

Imagine I am assigning you a part of the RFP project. I tell you, "Once you have that all written up be sure to print it on green paper before you turn it in to the project manager."

Are you imagining doing it? Can you see yourself buying the paper? Then, did you see yourself putting the green paper in the printer? Why is it always painful to switch paper stock in the printer tray, am I right? Now you go back to the computer, print your section on the green paper. Then you walk the stack to the PM to deliver your portion of the project. You leave feeling good. Phew, one more thing off your to do list!

Imagine your surprise when the PM calls upset! She accuses you of not following the instructions. She says you said you understood and you certainly didn't come asking any questions. All the while...you are trying to figure out what you did incorrectly?

She explains you used the wrong paper. You say you KNOW for sure you used green paper. You printed it and delivered it yourself. She explains you used the WRONG green. She wanted the light green paper not the bright green paper. You can hear the "duh" invisibly hanging in the air.

So, what's your green? The green YOU imagined before I started using specifics like "light" and "bright".

Take that one step further, WHY did you choose THAT green?

Did you think lime green? Maybe your best friend has a lime green armchair at their house that you see every time you go over there.

Or maybe you thought, forest green like the vivid green of pine trees in the mountains that you love to go hiking throughout each summer.

Or maybe, like the example, you thought of Kelly green. A bright medium green color because your favorite socks are Kelly green.

You see it, right? It is not enough to tell people what to do. For success in business, we MUST allow space for meaning, intention and understanding

Meaning can be qualified by giving more specifics or examples. "use light green paper"

Intention can be clarified by detailing reasoning. "for ease of reading the black print"

Understanding can be agreed upon through offering of your expected result and a space for questions!

"This will allow your section to stand out and still be legible. Can I get that by Friday at noon? Please give me a quick call today if you have any questions or cannot accommodate the deadline."

Telling a person what to do is NOT enough.

A kick ass Boss (whether the business owner, a project manager or a team lead) allows the space through access and time to allow an agreed understanding of the instruction to get the results we are INTENDING to receive.

If you can allow that each person has different experiences, (say, with the color green), then we have to allow that others can interpret the meaning of your communications differently than you intend. Without creating this dialogue, company culture and space to ask for, allow and expect questions we are dooming our business to inevitable frustrations, redundancy and EXPENSE!

Always ask if there are any questions, comments or conflicts you need to know about now. Questions are not usually about either side trying to ridicule or challenge authority; they are literally team members looking to achieve success. Employees WANT to do the job correctly. They really do want it to be right. Give them the time and validity to question your instructions. That IS a boss action!

Talmar Anderson,
Hiring & Management Expert
Boss Actions

***

Yes, Talmar!!

This goes for so many different aspects in the RFP process. Not only useful for managing your response team, but also something to keep in mind when you are writing your response.

Remembering that each evaluator will be envisioning a different color green will help you think through how to best paint the picture.

DO MORE OF THIS

4.14. Wrap It Up

Once the proposal goes out the door, we love to put it behind us. Sometimes we have to because it's time to work on the next one; or, we're just so happy to get it out the door that we run far, far away.

BUT, having a wrap-up process will help ensure a few things:

1. **Document lessons learned** while they're still fresh in your mind. Every single proposal response comes with lessons learned. Don't overlook those. Have a team meeting (even 15 minutes will go a long way!) to discuss openly what worked, what didn't work, what you need more of, what you need less of. Have someone taking notes and put these in a "Lessons Learned" document that can be accessible to all team members.

2. **Document your results.** Track wins and losses, response time, specific challenges, roadblocks, resource usage. And remember, we give you a tracking sheet for this in The RFP Success™ Kit.

3. **Add to your content library** those write-ups from this specific response that were especially strong so you can easily access them for the next response. This will save you a lot of time for the next response.

By now you've figured out that I love checklists and templates! And we have one in The RFP Success™ Institute for the entire wrap-up process, too.

Don't make this a long, hard process. Stay on track. Find easy ways to document, use the same agenda each time, assign a scribe, and know how you are going to use that information.

One last thing: feed your team. You can schedule a lunch meeting with your team to accomplish all of the above. Feed them a nice meal to thank them for their efforts and they're going to be much more productive in this post-proposal process.

The Snapshot

Key Takeaways

This section gives you a lot of opportunity to hone your process and approach so that things run smoothly and you don't waste time and effort.

My goal here is to help you win more business, and we've already established that you can't win just by throwing together a bunch of bids every year.

Resources

The Resources available to you from this chapter include:

From The RFP Success™ Kit, you can download:

- The Checks and Balances Checklist
- The Tracking Sheet
- The Opportunity Scorecard Checklist

The RFP Success™ Institute has you covered with:

- A debrief process template
- Tracking training

Chapter 5.

Love Sales Or Lose Business (And Yes, RFPs Are A Selling Mechanism)

I will keep harping on another obvious here, but you are indeed selling when you're responding to RFPs. Selling warrants its own section because it's one of those things that we seem to want to avoid. No avoiding. The strategies in this section will help you hit the selling angle head on but from a place of authenticity, not ickiness.

Embrace sales or lose business. Your choice

5.1. Sell, Dammit!

Such an appropriate first chapter for this section, because this is what it's all about! We respond to RFPs because we want to get more business (which means we have to sell more business).

That RFP response that you're crafting is nothing more than a sales opportunity. Plain and simple. It's a written sales call.

We often lose sight of that. And if you hate hearing that, tough. Get over it.

And here's more truth.

An RFP response is only a tool in the selling process; often times a necessary tool, but it isn't the only tool.

It surrounds the other pieces of the sales puzzle – namely, strategy and relationship-building. We'll dive deeper into that topic in another chapter.

When we are selling, we are providing a solution to a want or a need. Our potential client has a problem that they need solved. It is our job to show them how we will provide the best solution for their problem.

The first rule of thumb: Think in terms of a win-win solution. We want to win the business, but we also want Reality Rich to win. We want to provide the best opportunity for him to get the best result (and if that's not what you want, this book isn't going to help you!).

Second rule of thumb: Keep the end solution - the outcome - in mind. You are selling the solution, making it much more about what Reality Rich believes he needs, and less about what you know he needs.

Also, you are selling the *why* of your company. You have to convince them that you are the person/company that they can trust to give them the solution they need. They don't want to hire the wrong person. It's your job to show them that you're the right fit. And yes, it's about the fact that you have the expertise to get it done. But get this – they really don't care about you; they care that you aren't going to screw them over; they care that you can give them what they need. They care about the outcome first and foremost. Of course, they also want to like and trust you. And they need to understand how your expertise is going to help them. But they first need to believe you can help them.

5.2. Create A Proposal Promise

Before you start freaking out, thinking I'm telling you to make guarantees, that's not what a proposal promise is about. Think of your proposal promise as a theme that you will weave throughout your proposal so your client will get a very clear picture of that theme.

This promise will be based on your prospect's pain point(s) and showcases the outcome they will get by working with you.

This proposal promise is a "statement", not a dissertation - meaning, one clean crisp statement that is one sentence long. We're coming back to Simple. Specific. Succinct. It's all about discipline.

If there's only *one thing* that you want them to walk away from the proposal with, what is that one thing? *That* becomes your promise.

Think of it as a brand promise. You see these all the time whether you know it or not:

iPod: 10,000 songs in your pocket

Geico: 15 minutes or less can save you 15% or more on car insurance.

Hilton: Get more from your getaway.

A great brand promise is bold and clear and has a definable outcome. They challenge the status quo and get to the emotion of their clients. They are measurable and meaningful.

You're essentially creating the same thing. Remember earlier when I told you that we have to hear something 3 to 7 times before it really sinks in? That's why you want to create a proposal promise that you can weave throughout the proposal. You want to weave it in no less than 7 times. And use the formula that I shared earlier – Simple + Specific + Succinct – to really allow it to sink in with your readers.

Building a proposal promise does several things:

1. It helps to guide your writers to focus on that as a theme so the proposal reads consistently;

2. It gives the buyer(s) something to sink their teeth into and to really remember about you;

3. It helps you stand out and be memorable.

Let's go back to the examples above. Which ones do you think would resonate most after hearing it several times?

iPod: Put all of your favorite music on one external data storage device that you can easily carry with you.

or

10,000 songs in your pocket.✓

Geico: We can help you save up to 15% on your car insurance, and when you call us, we don't want to waste your time. We will get you off the phone in 15 minutes or less.

or

15 minutes or less can save you 15% or more on car insurance. 

Hilton: We have thousands of properties worldwide with multiple amenities that help you create the best experience for your money.

or

Get more from your getaway.

One of the best things to do is go back to your last three proposals and think about what proposal promise you could have assigned to those. That will help guide you to create a perfect Proposal Promise for your next response.

5.3. Give It Some Eye Candy

To piggy back on my "don't be boring" soapbox in an earlier chapter, here are some ways that you can really make your proposal pop from a visual perspective.

Include purposeful graphics. Don't include graphics just to include graphics. There has to be a purpose to each graphical element. Ask yourself what message you want each graphic to convey to the reader. What is the one key takeaway from that graphic?

Include clean and simple graphs. Do not get over-complicated with graphs. Clean, simple, and colorful will go a long way to making your proposal more readable. A graph should be able to capture attention in 2-3 seconds. If it doesn't, your reader will cruise on by.

Include call-outs. A call-out is a small colorful box that highlights a simple key point. Use these throughout your proposal for important quotes or small pieces of information. They will ensure that your prospect sees those important points, and it also makes your proposal more visually interesting. A call-out box should include:

- A bold statement that will smack 'em between the eyes and get them to want *that*. Less about *you*, more about an outcome. Please don't include a call-out that says what year you were founded. No one cares.
- A relevant teaching point, something they might not know, but that will peak their interest and increase your credibility.

Pay attention to white space. White space means that you have more white than black on a type-written page. In other words, less words. If there is too much black (aka writing), your reader can get bored, overwhelmed, confused and lost. White space wins.

To get more white space, use bullets, shorter paragraphs, diagrams, and tables to break up the writing.

If you're describing a process, break it out into steps rather than writing it into one large paragraph. Better yet, lay out the high-level steps into a graphic and then write up more detail in the summary.

Visual appeal is friendly, and your readers - especially those like Reality Rich - will appreciate friendly (just don't forget that content matters too, of course).

5.4. Make It Experiential

Today's world requires us to share stories. People want relatability almost more than they want experience.

You want to take your readers on a journey. You want them to *feel* what it's going to be like to work with you.

Here are some things you can include in your proposal that will contribute to that journey:

Stories. We are most definitely in the storytelling era. You can't pick up a business book, read anything about sales and marketing, or hear a business guru speech without someone touting how important storytelling is. Why? Because it goes back to the relatability. But frankly, it goes beyond just relatability, it's how we remember things.

If you create the right kind of story, you can capture your reader's memories and feelings to really draw them in. A story paints a picture that allows us to see it come to life. That makes the reading experience sooooo much more interesting and intriguing, and it makes us want it more. Stories engage our senses and emotions and bring forth how we want our lives to be. There is actually science behind this! So tell stories that draw your audience in and allow them to feel what it's going to be like to work with you.

Case studies. Case studies have a beginning (the situation), a middle (the approach), and an end (the outcome). You have to have all three of these pieces to create a compelling case study. But these can be powerful because they are stories. Case studies show the reader how you can help them because you have helped someone in a similar situation as themselves. Relate prior client successes back to your prospects' specific pain and challenges. Be as quantifiable as possible.

Testimonials. Provide testimonial quotes and letters from happy clients. You can also give them a specific format you want these testimonials in so you ensure they are giving you quantifiable feedback that will make the right kind of impact when included in your proposals.

Embed a video. Video is a huge power play if you are willing to go there. Embedding a video into your proposal is the hidden cream in the cupcake. There's no better way to build trust and rapport than an in-person meeting; the second best way is via video, because they can see your face and get to know your personality. A video showcasing the team, with a message from each key team member, would certainly help you stand out!

Take them on a journey. Show them you understand their pain and can see from their perspective. You can tell them, or you can show them. The latter is going to go much further. Prove to them that you have the solution. Help them see and feel how things will be better when working with you.

Remember, the clients' perception is the clients' reality. It's your job to create that perception.

It's President's weekend, the offices are closed for the long weekend, so Reality Rich decides to take a road trip. As he's driving down the highway, perfectly content, he starts seeing billboards for an upcoming restaurant.

At this point, Reality Rich isn't thinking about food. He's just passing time by reading the billboards.

The first picture is just about the restaurant, nothing too intriguing. He notices it, but nothing registers.

Second billboard shows a huge, juicy, loaded burger. Cheese oozing between two juicy meat patties; crunchy pickles stacked below the toasted bun; crispy bacon hanging over the side (hungry yet??). All of a sudden, Reality Rich starts to feel hungry. The thought hadn't crossed his mind until now.

The third billboard shows a very attractive woman eating this exact same burger with a big smile on her face, looking extremely content. The message on the billboard reads, "Next exit!" Reality Rich is now insatiable, so he takes the next exit and heads to this restaurant to get his burger.

This is suggestive marketing at its best. Again, seems like a far cry from an RFP response, but it's not. Those billboards conjured a feeling, an emotion in Reality Rich. They told him something he didn't already know — that he was hungry and that he had to have a burger. At that point, his subconscious took over and he knew he had to have that burger. That is the exact emotion that you want to evoke in your readers. Show them they want what only you have to offer.

5.5. Smack 'Em Between The Eyes

The world is a busy place these days, it's imperative for you to stand out. These five strategies will help you smack your potential clients between the eyes to get your message across.

Be solution-focused - your client doesn't care about the product or service that you're selling. They care that you can solve their want or need. Speak their language, speak to their pain, and you'll grab their attention. You want them to feel like you're talking directly to them and this particular issue.

Multiple mentions - Telling your potential client something once likely isn't going to resonate the first time. Studies show that it takes 3 to 7 times hearing something for it to really sink in. Don't be afraid to repeat yourself.

Attention-grabbing - You have 2 to 3 seconds to grab your client's attention before they drift off. They are reading multiple proposals, maybe even while multi-tasking. What is going to make you stand out? Be bold to grab their attention.

Confusion free - A confused mind doesn't buy. Avoid offering too many options, too much text, and difficult theories. Make it easy for them to understand what you are offering and what it will be like to work with you.

KISS - Keep it super simple - Your potential client doesn't know what you know. You've got to find a way to simplify so that anyone can understand what you're saying.

5.6. Show Your Personality

At the end of the day, we all want to do business with people we like. No one wants to work with someone they don't like, or whose personality rubs them the wrong way. The more you can show them who you are so they get an opportunity to like you, the better. It also builds on the trust factor, because they will feel like they know you.

Showcase your company's personality, or team members personalities. Let them know who you are, what your culture is, and what it will be like to work with you.

Some proposals will give you the opportunity to be more creative than others. Obviously, you've got to know your audience. But don't be afraid to show who you are.

We were working with a client on a presentation for a large food manufacturer. The food manufacturer clearly stated that they wanted to know how our client connected to their overall mission. They wanted to know about the team members assigned to the project. And they wanted our client to showcase that they understood the overall culture of their company.

Because this was a confidential bid, for the purposes of this story we'll say they were submitting a bid to provide a service to a cupcakery.

Our client was so in their head, unconscious to what their prospect was asking for, very internally focused. They were about to miss the opportunity to really showcase their personality when we were brought in to help.

Now tell me, which one of these (over-simplified) write-ups would you remember more:

1

We were established in 1962, in Tucson, Arizona. We have a long-standing reputation in Arizona as one of the premier providers of xyz products. Our customer service scores are always extremely high and we have a very large repeat customer base.

2

We started our business in the valley the same decade as xyz bakery. In fact, several members of our proposed team have fond childhood memories of your bakery.

Stan, who will be managing this project, used to go to the bakery every Sunday after church with his family. He always got the same thing – the glazed donut. He is so fond of your bakery that he has carried on the tradition with his own family (insert picture of Stan and his family at a table in the bakery).

Okay, you get the picture.

So, are you going to be the one wearing the drab beige suit with the non-descript tie? Or are you going to be the one that walks in with the tailored suit and an eye-catching tie? Your choice.

5.7. Connect With Your Target

If you're someone who is going to say it's too hard, it's impossible, etc. to connect with public sector targets, or to connect with the big shots at the large corporations, then let me tell you right now, you're going to fail. Good lord.

Yes, that's blunt, but of course you've figured out by now that I'm a pretty direct girl.

Is it harder to connect with buyers in the RFP space? Maybe. Probably. But just because it's harder doesn't mean it isn't just as important.

You'll have to get creative.

This is one of my favorite topics because I hear *all the time* how difficult it is to reach the buyers. And, of course, once a procurement hits the streets, particularly in the government space, you are prohibited from contacting them outside of the Q&A period or bidder's conference. That's why doing the research and really understanding your targets *before* the procurement is so essential.

When there is not a procurement on the streets and you have identified a company as a green light or yellow light target, you should have a plan of action for how you are going to continue to stay in touch with them to build the relationship.

- **Show up where they are.** There are government procurement conferences, association and industry events, networking events. You have to ask them, or ask around, to find out where they hang out. Then show up and start connecting. There are a lot of Reality Riches out in the world looking to connect back with you.

- **Share a meal.** Invite them to coffee or lunch. This is likely more suitable to the corporate environment versus government, but you never know until you ask. Offer to buy, but they likely can't take you up on that. Though they will appreciate the offer.
- **Send them valuable information.** Don't just reach out to try and sell them. Send them articles that might help them in their job, connect them to resources that will make their lives easier. We *all* love when someone shares something that makes our lives easier.
- **Ask for introductions.** Who do you know that might be able to make an introduction?
- **Use social media.** Have you connected to them on LinkedIn or other appropriate social platforms? Is there an association group on social that you can join to mingle with them?
- **Call them.** Simply just pick up the phone and call.

No matter what it is, stay in touch and build that relationship.

When I talk to buyers who are hard to reach, they say a simple hand-written note can go a long way. They also say that they want to be communicated to regularly - maybe not weekly, but once a month or once a quarter to just remind them via a simple email that you are out there. It helps them to remember who you are and what you offer. They are juggling a lot of plates, so don't assume that just because you've met them once or you've submitted a proposal in the past that they will remember you. Likely not. Help them remember that you exist and that you are an ideal solution to their challenge(s).

And please remember that a relationship is a two-way connection, a conversation, a win-win for both parties. It can't be all about you. Add value, don't just send them a note with a stack of business cards and pedal your wares. You're building a relationship here.

I once had a conversation with a client who was frustrated that a large corporation wasn't hiring her company. She had spent some time with this company, provided her capabilities statement, and sat back to wait for business to come rolling in.

Hmm.... that's not really how it works.

We were working with her on her go-to-market strategy and dividing her prospects up to assign action tasks to them. This company was listed as a prospect, but she said no action needed to be taken. As I dug in a little further, she simply said, "They already know what we do, we don't need to keep calling on them." When I pushed harder, she said: "We gave them a capabilities brochure, they should know what we do!"

To be brutally honest, that was a very short-sighted comment, because that presumes the buyer doesn't have much on their plate or doesn't get a gazillion capabilities brochures on a weekly basis. It presumes they are going to remember you over every other vendor they communicate with, not to mention in the sea of other tasks they have on their plate.

It's in your best interest to continue to stay in front of them. Be persistent, just don't be pesky!

Also, stop using the excuse that the contract won't come up for bid for another three years or five years. If they are a green or yellow light target, you should be building that relationship that entire time. Yes, it could possibly take that long. But are you in this for the long haul or not? It might feel like it's far into the future, but you want to position yourself perfectly when its time. And as we all know, time goes by fast!

If there is a live bidder's conference, you want to attend. And you're not just attending to scope out the competition, or to be there as a requirement, or ask questions. Use this as an opportunity to connect with the people who are live and in the room.

I recently heard of a study that was done on flight attendants and their connection with the passengers. The essence of it was, as people are coming onto the plane, those that made direct eye contact with the flight attendants and those that were well groomed made more of a positive impact on the crew and were more likely to get more positive attention and a higher level of service. No words were said, it was simply based on outer appearance and body language.

Call it what you want – judgmental, bias, etc. But non-verbal communication is powerful.

❑ Don't Just Take My Word For It...

How many times do you go to a bidder's conference, you sign in, find a seat, and take out your notebook to start taking notes? You're on a mission and you're not paying any attention to human connection.

The thing is, body language and projection are powerful.

Expert contributor, Tish Times, recently gave my radio show listeners a great piece of advice. If you are at a bidder's conference, don't just sign your name in and go sit down. Shake the hand of the buyers that are in the room, making direct eye contact with them. Hand them your business card, smile, and let them know you look forward to the opportunity to work with them. You will be surprised at how far this can go in building that rapport. They will remember you.

Such a perfect segway.....

Meet Tish Times as she shares more golden nuggets when it comes to building relationships before, during and after the RFP process.

***

I love connecting people; so much so that I run a company specializing in creating connection. I teach people how to network and sell by building lasting relationships.

My very first job was with a temporary staffing company. I thrived on connecting eager job seekers with companies in desperate need of the skill set they brought to the table. I thought creating connection was easy; even fun. I found, however, that connection is not the strong suit of every professional. Many business leaders struggle to connect with the decision makers with whom they need to engage.

As a staffing professional and later the owner of a staffing company, an important part of my work was to answer RFPs. Often, I heard colleagues say that talking to contracting officers was off limits. Although I know there are some parameters that must be respected, I did not completely agree. I made it my mission to learn ways to connect with these untouchables while regarding the rules. I learned that if treated them like people, instead of off-limits figureheads, they would respond.

My interaction with contracting officers and other influencers helped my company secure local, state, and federal contracts. Connecting wasn't as difficult as you might assume, and these relationships were essential to my winning these bids. Here are some of the strategies that I used:

- ***Attend matchmaking events.** Government agencies often host or attend matchmaking events making it easy for bidders to meet the contracting team. They aren't always free; however, it is worth every minute and dollar you may spend to travel, wait in line, and brave the crowd to shake these officials' hands.*
- ***Participate during bidder's conferences.** Please note, I said participate, not just attend. Bidder's conferences may not always be mandatory, but you do yourself a disservice if you opt out of these opportunities. You want the contracting team to know your name. Come armed with intelligent questions, notebook in hand, and be prepared to take notes as they share their wisdom.*
- ***Pick up the telephone.** When allowed, make connection with the person or team who will be reviewing your response. Remain professional and don't cross any lines, but do your best to get to know the people in the agency. When your response crosses their desk, you don't want it to be just another form they must review. (And when I couldn't get a response, I would send a question via Fed-Ex. Everyone opens a package that seems important.)*

- ***If you are not awarded, don't shut down communication.*** *If you've done a great job connecting and did everything else right but still did not win - you may have an opportunity to request an out brief. Ask what the winning bid had over yours. Find out what you might do better next time to have a better chance. I've seen instances where the selected company did not perform well or needed support and another company was given an opportunity to come on board. Nurture the connection no matter what.*

Tish Times, CEO
Tish Times Networking & Sales Training

***

As always, such great advice and insight, Tish. Thank you!

Ok, I realize this can be overwhelming.
But trust me, it's actually very simple.
You just must have a game plan.

To help you get your game plan going, check out
The RFP Success™ Kit
and print out the Monthly Calendar
to help you create your own connection strategy.

We already know that Reality Rich is a social butterfly, so of course he's out and about networking at industry events. He meets a lot of people. Last month, he met several people who implement cloud technology solutions.

First up was Lola. Lola had a great smile and walked right up to Reality Rich, looked him in the eyes and shook his hand. She asked him what he did for a living, what he likes to do for fun, and what other networking events he attends. She listened well and seemed genuinely interested, and he took note of that.

After he talked for a while answering her questions, Reality Rich asked Lola what she did for a living. Lola responded with a question: "well, Rich, does your agency currently use cloud technology?"

Rich was thrilled that he knew what she was talking about and answered with a resounding "Yes!". Lola went a little deeper and asked, "Have you or anyone in your agency ever had any challenges with retrieving your data from the cloud?" Reality Rich laughed, as he proceeded to tell Lola about an exact problem that they recently had with that. Lola let him know that that's the exact problem that her company solves for — making sure that doesn't happen and that the team can easily and quickly retrieve their data so they don't lose productivity, and they don't get stressed or frustrated.

Reality Rich thought to himself, "Ah, wouldn't that be nice — no loss of productivity and less frustration and stress? Sign me up!" They talked for a little longer, Reality Rich asked for Lola's card, and off he went to continue his networking.

Next up was Tim. Tim walked up to Reality Rich, also confident with a big smile, and firmly shook Rich's hand. A big personality, Tim immediately handed Reality Rich his business card and proceeded to talk about what he does. "You know, dude, cloud computing is where it's at. If you're not using cloud computing, you're falling behind. You're missing the boat. The elasticity and self-service provisioning alone create an ideal environment. We could do private cloud, public cloud, hybrid. There are so many options. Give me a call and let's talk!" And Tim was off to his next conquest.

Last up with Tiffany. Tiffany is shy so she waited for others to come to her. Being the social being that Reality Rich is, he saw her standing alone so he headed over to start up a conversation. Tiffany didn't look Reality Rich in the eyes and she was very soft-spoken. When Reality Rich asked her what she did, she reached into her purse and pulled out a business card, handed it to him and meekly said, "cloud technology".

Reality Rich followed up with a second question: "Tell me more, how do you do that?" Tiffany, again with a short answer, stated, "Well, we can implement a public cloud solution, a private cloud solution, or a hybrid." Again, no questions for Reality Rich, so he tucked her business card behind Tim's in his pocket and decided to move on.

Back in the office the next day, Reality Rich opens his email to find a note from Lola. She was following up to say she enjoyed meeting him and thanked him for sharing the story about his frustrating cloud technology moment. She also extended an invitation for them to meet for coffee in the next couple of weeks to further their conversation. Reality Rich immediately responded and they set up a coffee meet-up.

A great reminder of their conversation without throwing what she does in his face.

One month later, Reality Rich is pulled into an RFP for —you guessed it — cloud computing! Which one of the people above do you think he reached out to share the RFP with? And which one do you think he would advocate for internally?

Impressions matter; relationships matter. Showing genuine interest, asking questions to make the conversation relatable, and authentic follow-up put Lola in the winner's circle.

Learn from Lola. Be Lola.

5.8. Show Them You Want It

You have to step up and demonstrate to the client that you want the business. Not from the perspective of being desperate, but from a place of true commitment and belief that you are the right vendor.

Tell them you want it. Tell them why you want it. Show them why you are the right partner and how you are the only partner they should even be considering.

Even more importantly, do *not* assume they know this. Especially if it's your current contract and you're having to bid because they require a bid process, do not assume they know you want to keep the contract. Assume nothing.

Go after the business like it is the most important client ever - because frankly, it is. They all are the most important.

If you're bidding to win a contract that you're the incumbent on, remind them of why you are their partner now; show them you want it back; don't let any sliver of light in for someone else to steal it away from you.

The team and I were recently doing a proposal review for a client that had responded to a public-sector RFP for a contract that they currently held. In other words, they were the incumbent. It was theirs to lose.

They had had this contract for several iterations, so they were embedded. They knew the client well and felt they had a solid relationship. There was no reason to believe the client wasn't happy with their work.

But guess what? They lost.

One of their competitors had done their homework, had been working on building the relationship, and showcased in their bid that they wanted this business more than our client did.

When they contacted the client for a debrief, the client hemmed and hawed and finally told them that the new vendor just seemed to want it more. They had new innovative ideas, they "listened" more to what they RFP was asking for, and they proved that they would make the transition smooth and seamless.

After this experience, our client engaged us to review their response and the winning bidder's response. And it was very clear – the winning bidder most definitely showed that they wanted it more. Our client had rested on their laurels. They didn't show in the least that they wanted to retain this business. They were in their head, got way too technical, spent a lot of time reminding them of their processes and expertise. But they did nothing to make their current client feel like they were special.

Lesson learned.

Don't be afraid to tell them that you want to work with them. Don't do this from a place of desperation, but from a place of passion.

Make bold statements about why you want to work with them.

If you are the incumbent, remind them what you do for them and how you partner with them. Remind them about the results you've gotten for them. Talk about why the team loves working with them, and any stand-out relationships that you have. Don't write like you don't know them.

5.9. Create Value

Creating value in your proposal goes above and beyond the hard dollar costs. It's about showing how the benefit of your service outweighs the actual cost.

Cost is a hard number. The challenge is, particularly when you are providing a service, cost is relative. If you're going to charge less than your competitor, but it's going to take you twice as long or you aren't delivering as much, your competitor actually has more value. You might win because you have a lower cost, but you aren't adding as much value in the end.

Value is also what your customer believes the product or service is worth to them.

The bigger their pain, the higher value they place on the solution.

How can you add value over and above hard costs?

Consider these options:

- Give them something no one else can give them - a proprietary process or system, an in-house technology, a patented product
- Access to something they don't have now - a certain skillset, additional team members, resources
- A unique way to make their lives easier

- A higher level of productivity or efficiency (this is actually the *best* way!); it's not just about bottom-line costs, how do you create more efficiencies (through a process of some sort?) or increased productivity (through training or technology?) that will actually affect costs in a positive way?

Everyone thinks it's about price. That's becoming less and less the case. Clients want value more than they want price. Again, Reality Rich needs to find the *right* solution or he's going to look like a complete tool to his boss.

Knowing the value that your company adds beyond just bottom-line price, and showcasing that in your response, will cause the readers to take notice.

5.10. Sell The Hole, Not The Drill

"Features tell, benefits sell."

Features are about us, our service or product, while a benefit is about the client and what they will get by working with us. In short, the benefit is about the outcome.

We want to spend a lot more time talking about the benefits of working with us (aka the end results), and less about the features. Clients only care about the features once they believe you can solve their problem.

It's the classic drill and hole analogy. People don't buy a drill because they want or need a drill; they buy a drill because they want or need a hole. The benefit of the drill is that it provides a hole (or, in short, the want/need). The feature of the drill is that it's cordless, or it's got a certain level of horsepower, etc.

Clearly delineate between features and benefits and learn to "sell" the benefits in your RFP response. Talk 80% benefits, 20% features.

Check out these examples:

Feature: A small consulting firm that offers personalized attention.
Benefit: Access to senior staff when you need them.

Feature: Batteries included.
Benefit: Product is ready to use.

Feature: Free home delivery.
Benefit: Save time.

Get the picture? How can you turn your company's features into benefits?

5.11. Tell Stories

We've already talked about sharing the experience and taking your clients on a journey. I want to go a little deeper into storytelling as it relates to RFPs, because the more stories you can tell, the better picture you'll be painting for your client.

But hear this......

Telling stories is *not* an opportunity to talk about you and your company even more. The stories need to be relevant about past experiences and client successes that relate specifically to the solution you are providing.

Here's your storytelling checks and balances. Use these as a guide when crafting your stories:

- What do you want them to know?
- What do you want them to feel?
- What do you want them to do?
- How does all of this relate to their desired outcome?

You're essentially reverse engineering the story. Start with the end in mind so your story paints the right picture.

5.12. Know Your Prospect

This chapter ties very closely to connecting with your prospect. The more you can connect with them, the more overall knowledge you'll have about them.

Remember that Proposal Promise (pg. 122)? You won't be able to create one if you don't know the prospect and what they really need.

Here are some key things you need to know about your prospect:

- What is causing them to go out to bid?
- What challenges have they had in this arena in the past?
- What type of external or stakeholder pressure are they receiving on this project?
- Was there a specific event that led to this need?

Knowing the "Reality Rich" of your prospect is part of selling; the more you know, the easier the sale, because you understand how to speak their language and you understand what is driving their need.

Understanding the issues will make your response so much more powerful!

The Snapshot

Key Takeaways

The premise of this section is simple - don't be afraid to sell. You've got to embrace sales, or you're going to lose business. And yes, RFPs are absolutely a sales opportunity, a written sales call. And you want to stand out from the rest and make the best showing possible.

Resources

Make sure you download the **Connection Calendar** from The RFP Success™ Kit to keep you on track with your Connection Strategy.

Chapter 6.

Watch Out For These 'Cliff-Edgers' That Will Have You Hitting Rock Bottom

It's pretty easy to fall into some of the same traps over and over again. Even if we tell ourselves we'll be better next time, the next time rolls around and the timelines are tight, there are a million other things on our plates, and things fall through the cracks.

These are the things that you really need to watch out for because they are simple fixes but can be big disasters.

WATCH OUT FOR

6.1. Running Out Of Time

Managing the timeline of a response is a huge part of a successful response. Whoever is tasked with managing the response is tasked with managing the due date and making sure things get done on time.

Two words: Reverse Engineer.

You should always, *always* create a Response Calendar (and of course we have a sample for you in The RFP Success™ Kit!). When we manage responses for our clients, the first thing we do (after reading the RFP) is create the Response Calendar.

And guess what the first thing is that goes into the Response Calendar?

Yep, the due date.

Put the due date in first and then reverse engineer everything else.

When you do this, it helps you better manage the timeline. Because it is so easy to lose track of time. And it's so easy for the other team members to not have a clue what it takes down the home stretch of an RFP response.

Always watch out for these things that may trip you up and cause you to run out of time:

- **Oblivious contributors.** Those who contribute at a high level and are never involved in the finalization of an RFP response have absolutely no idea what it takes to get it over the finish line. That's why we create the calendar and make sure they have very defined due dates.

- **Unforeseen challenges.** Technology glitches. Broken down copy machines. Human error. Weather. Sickness. Traffic. Family emergencies. *Ish happens. Every. Single. Time. Put a little padding in for these types of things and be prepared to troubleshoot.
- **Final changes, formatting, final look.** This takes time if you want to do it right. And this is the piece that tends to get pushed because no one really values it until it disqualifies them. Watch out for slippage here. It's an important step that you can't afford to skip.

WATCH OUT FOR

6.2. Me! Me! Me!

Surprise!

Your RFP response is not about you.

No, really.

Tough pill to swallow, but the proposal must be focused on the client. First focused on their pain or challenge, then on the solution that you can provide. Stop tooting your own horn until it's truly time to toot your own horn!

You've likely heard the acronym WIIFT – What's In It For Them.

Stop talking about your expertise and address their challenges.

Tell them how they will benefit (aka, what's in it for them) from working with you. You really have to take a step back and put yourself in their shoes and think about it from *their* perspective.

You're passionate about what you do, I get it. You love what you offer. You *know* you can help people.

But the tough love is this: *Your prospect doesn't care about you or your product or service.* What they care about is if you can solve their need or want.

It's a fine line, and we are often too close to our own stuff to realize that we keep talking about *ourselves* and are not talking about what will resonate with the potential client.

Here's a {masked} example from a recent RFP that we reviewed:

> Their answer:
> *We have been around since 1972 and use only the highest quality ingredients in our beverages. We have a 30,000 square foot facility where we produce our beverages and we create new flavors each month.*
>
> Revised answer:
> *Our beverages provide a unique flavor experience for your customers that they won't find anywhere else. You are able to create an experience for your diners that want them coming back for more, and an opportunity to increase your average check amount.*

When you're responding to RFPs (or preparing any sort of proposal, for that matter), this is hugely important. This is how you're going to smack 'em between the eyes (remember pg. 130?) so they pay attention to your message.

Consider these examples.

You don't buy a Coke because you want a Coke. You buy a Coke because you are thirsty or craving the sweet flavor. If Coke focused on itself, its commercials would all be about the ingredients in Coke, or how the Coke is made. But their commercials are generally about pouring the Coke into a cold frosty mug to, or other ways that appeal to the feeling that you get when you drink a Coke.

Now, you may be thinking that an RFP isn't a Coke commercial. It isn't, but it's the same basic premise. You have to appeal to what your client wants or needs in order to capture their attention.

Stop making it all about you.

Many years ago, I drove a BMW 325i with a license plate cover that said, "It's All About Me!" Now, most people that know me would not consider me to be a self-absorbed egotist, it was just a fun license place cover loosely based on a line from a movie – Overboard. The movie starred Goldie Hawn as an elitist yacht owner who had an entire staff at her beck and call. She's in the middle of a tiff with her carpenter who is calling her out on her entitled attitude when she blurts out, "I'm not bored, everybody wants to be me!"

That line just cracked me up, certainly in the context of the movie (it's an oldie but goodie, so if you haven't seen it, check it out!).

Okay, so back to the license plate. I personally thought it was cute and funny. However, I soon learned that the impression it made on those who didn't know me – especially attached to a BMW – was not favorable. There was a guy that I worked with that I had a huge crush on and it turns out he decided he wasn't interested in me based solely on that license plate cover. Hmph.

What does that have to do with RFPs?

First impressions stick, and perception is reality. From dating to RFPs, human behavior doesn't change.

WATCH OUT FOR

6.3. Copying And Pasting

We're constantly looking for ways to leverage our old information to save time. I am a huge proponent of that. However, you have to be very careful when it comes to repurposing information.

In a perfect world, you will redact client names before storing content for repurposing purposes. But let's be realistic - unless you have a dedicated team member for that, it's not always possible.

But BE WARE!

If you copy and paste from an old proposal, someone has to go through with a fine-tooth comb to make sure you aren't referencing an old client.

And it goes beyond just the client name. It's easy to do a "search and replace" on a client name. Where you can get tripped up is client-specific departments, verbiage, program names, city or state references.

Whenever we work with a client, we have a **Checks and Balances Checklist** that we use at the end of a response. And guess what's on it? This exact thing. (and btw, this checklist is also part of The RFP Success™ Kit so you don't have to miss a beat!)

I was talking to a buyer at a large utility provider here in my hometown. There are essentially two main companies that provide this type of utility, and they are both very well known. For the purposes of this story, let's call them U1 and U2 (no, I'm not talking about the band, I'm really referencing a utility company).

We're hanging out with a group of people and talking about RFP horror stories. I always love this conversation because I learn so much about what not to do that I can share with our clients. Buyer at

U1 told us about a time when they received a proposal from a bidder who had references to U2 all over the place. It was clear they had just copied and pasted from their response to U2 and forgot to go back and change the company name.

Yikes!

Guess what U1 did with that proposal? You guessed it..... right into the trash.

It was one of those awkward moments when everyone gasped as they listened to the story, then laughed, then you could see on everyone's face that they knew how easy it would be for that to happen to them.

Moral of the story? Be very careful when you copy and paste!

WATCH OUT FOR

6.4. 'We Can't Change' Syndrome

This is such a basic of human behavior. We have in our mind that things work a certain way, and it's sometimes hard to push ourselves to think that another way is possible.

The reason that this is so important when it comes to RFPs is that we can really get into a rhythm and process that seemingly works well.

But what if, just what if, [Drrrrrrrrrrrrrrrrum-roll]....

There was a better way?

Always be open to that. Don't change just for the sake of change but be open. If you can be open, you can continue to improve. I have yet to meet a client that has the perfect strategy, process, response when it comes to RFPs (or anything, really). There is always room for improvement.

We had a client come to us and they were struggling to win RFPs. After doing a proposal review, we were able to pinpoint many things that they needed to improve.

Next RFP, they lost. We did another review and found that they didn't incorporate any of our suggested changes. When I asked why, they said they didn't have time. Um, hello? Jaw drop!

Look, if you don't have time to make things right, you shouldn't be bidding. But that's another topic. Let's keep going with the story.....

We then suggested that for their next proposal, we provide a review of their draft proposal so we could help incorporate some of the key changes they needed to make. They were resistant to the timeline, so we put together their response calendar to show them how it could be done.

They didn't get it done in time. We didn't have time to review. They lost again.

Next proposal, same process. This time they made the time. And they won!

Here's the deal – is it worth losing over and over to keep doing things the same way?

We know for a fact that timelines can be re-managed. We do it all the time when clients that *are* willing to change give us enough time at the end to provide that review. They value it because they value winning over losing.

What about you – do you value winning over losing? Or are you going to refuse to change?

WATCH OUT FOR

6.5. Confusing Your Reader

A confused mind doesn't buy. If you confuse your reader, they're done. If you cause them to have to read a sentence or paragraph much more than one time, you've lost them. If you make them work too hard, they're out.

When was the last time you got excited to read something that didn't make any sense to you? Maybe you're someone who loves the challenge to figure it out, but you are in the minority.

Here are some things you can do to avoid confusing your reader:

- **Write in relatively short sentences.** There's nothing worse than a technical response that has one sentence as an entire paragraph (and I see this often!). Reality Rich will be annoyed and you'll lose him.
- **Turn processes into steps.** People will understand, "Step 1, Step 2, Step 3" better than they will understand, "First, we do this. After that, we do this. Then we continue on and do xyz."
- **Avoid using slang or industry jargon.** Assume no one knows.

Go back to the old tried and true: Simple. Specific. Succinct.

WATCH OUT FOR

6.6. Giving Them More Than They Asked For

An RFP response is overwhelming in and of itself. There's plenty of information that they are already requesting, there is no need for us to give them much more than that.

Your job is to win *this* RFP. Once you win, you can get in there and tell them more about what you do and how you can help. It's called upselling, or cross-selling. There is a time and a place, but it's not in the RFP.

Overwhelming your reader isn't any better than confusing your reader. They go hand in hand. Too much information and they will shut down.

The first non-hospitality RFP that I ever worked on was when I was a new employee at this large consulting firm. We were bidding on employee benefits brokerage services for a large local employer. This was a green-light target for us so we wanted to put our best foot forward.

I was part of the team only to help herd the cattle, format the response, keep an eye out on the requirements. I was not involved from a strategic or technical standpoint.

I remember sitting in a meeting with the team as they all talked about the cool things that we could include in our response: A copy of this dashboard, a brochure about this service that we offer, pictures of this, graphs of that. I remember scrambling to find where, in the RFP itself, any of this related. It didn't.

The team was in classic, "We Are Awesome!" mode and they wanted to showcase it all. They were giving the client so much more than they asked for.

Being the low man on the totem pole, I kept my mouth shut. Certainly they all knew better than me.

I was wrong.

As our response, we submitted three 4-inch binders. Let me say that again for full affect – THREE 4-inch binders. The first binder included our response, the other two binders included our attachments, most of which weren't relevant to what they were asking for.

We lost (you saw that coming, didn't you?).

I remember a couple of years later getting a chance to meet one of the evaluators in a social setting. We somehow started talking about this and they remembered our submittal. They never even looked at it. It was far too big and overwhelming that they disqualified us right out of the gate.

Seven copies of three 4-inch binders went directly into the trash.

Holy Schnikey. This is what we call the thud factor. If I feels like it's going to make a "thud", you may have too much information.

That was a great lesson learned.

WATCH OUT FOR

6.7. Not Giving Them What They Asked For

I know what you're thinking – why wouldn't you give them what they ask for?

You'd be surprised. And you'd be surprised that you probably do this without even knowing it.

Look, you're an expert at what you do. You can probably see more of what the client needs than they can see for themselves. You can often determine that what they think they need isn't going to solve their problem, and that they're asking for the wrong stuff.

You have to meet the client where they're at.

This is one of the reasons it's so great to have a relationship with the client before the RFP is released. Ideally, you want to help shape that RFP (actually, ideally you want them to just sole source the work to you, but that's a whole other conversation.) If you can provide input before the RFP, you can help your client see where they're at.

But once the RFP is released, you have two choices – meet them where they're at or decline to bid.

You can certainly ask clarifying questions to help guide them as I shared in an earlier story. But if you respond to what you want them to do versus what they believe they need, you're going to lose.

Reality Rich decided to have a party. He wants to show his appreciation to his clients by having a nice steak and lobster dinner for about 20 of his closest clients.

Reality Rich decided to hire a caterer, so he can tend to his guests during the actual party, rather than cooking. He talks to Kate the caterer, communicates his desire for steak and lobster, and they schedule the date.

On the day of his party, he notices that Kate the caterer doesn't have any steak and lobster; in fact, they're serving chicken and salmon. Reality Rich is ticked!

Kate the caterer decided to change the menu because she assumed that the clientele wanted to be slightly healthier. Kate the caterer also knew that there would be dancing, so she didn't want to weigh the guests down with a heavier dinner.

Kate the caterer was fired. Reality Rich wrote a bunch of bad reviews. Party over.

Kate the caterer may not have been wrong in her assumptions, but she was certainly wrong in her delivery of what the client wanted. This might be a simplistic way to look at it, but we see this type of thing all the time.

You may be able to see what the client really needs, but until the client sees that for themselves, you'll never get them to buy in. Meet them where they are until you have a live opportunity to shift their perspective.

Learn from Kate. Don't be Kate.

WATCH OUT FOR

6.8. Evaluation Criteria

Most RFPs will give you some sort of indication of the scoring or evaluation criteria. Right, we all know that.

But how can you best use that to your advantage?

First, let me state the obvious.

Pay attention to the evaluation criteria.

We can very easily get wrapped up in the RFP requirements, answering the technical questions, and herding the cats that we can lose track of what we will actually be scored on.

The evaluation criteria will give us clues. It tells us what's most important to our clients. A lot of times, you can also tell what their hot buttons are based on how their scoring criteria is set up and the verbiage they use. And at the very least, it helps us know where to put the most time and effort into the response.

All too many times I've seen people put so much time and attention into their experience when that section is worth only 5 out of 100 points. Sure, it's still important, but your level of effort needs to be in balance with the scoring criteria. And it will help keep you sane when you're trying to meet a tight deadline.

WATCH OUT FOR

6.9. Not Answering The Damn Question!

This goes into the category of "Obvious Chapters for $100, Alex."

My company reviews hundreds of proposals every year, and every single one falls into this trap. Every. Single. One.

This is also by far the most frequent complaint I get from buyers: *"How do we just get them to answer the damn question?!"*

Answer the question. That's it.

Answer their question.

Why the heck is this so hard?

Because we are moving at the speed of sound. We see what we want to see. We're juggling too many things, but someone has to slow down long enough to pay attention. The only saving grace here is that your competitors are probably making the exact same mistake.

I see two classic mistakes that happen – one, the responder just goes off on a tangent, focusing mostly on themselves and completely avoiding even the simplest of questions; and two, the question will really be seven questions disguised as one (I hate when that happens!).

A couple of strategies to help with these:

1. For the multi-part questions, create a table, or even sub-sections, for the response template that breaks the question out. You don't have to keep that format for the final response, but it helps you keep track of it and it helps your writers not miss anything;

2. Always have an objective reviewer assigned for this very specific reason.

3. Create an answer by simply reiterating their question.

The great thing is, this is pretty easy to fix. The **Checks and Balances Checklist** in the RFP Success™ Kit will set you up for success. No excuse to not pay attention and make it right!

WATCH OUT FOR

6.10. Team Burnout

We really do ask a lot of our proposal teams. Whether you have a large, dedicated team that works solely on proposals, or you have one-quarter of a person helping you crank these things out on occasion, there is huge opportunity for burn-out.

Deadlines are tight, there are a million moving pieces, there's always changes or roadblocks, the RFP itself is frustrating and confusing. The list goes on and on. The people working on responding to RFPs definitely don't have a 9 to 5 job. And for smaller companies, people are asked to help with RFPs on top of their already full-time technical role.

Having the right people in the role(s) who thrive in that kind of environment is hugely important, but even then, we're all susceptible to burnout.

What can you do to support, manage, and motivate your team, yourself included?

Here are some ideas that you can incorporate.

- Bring in a chair masseuse to give them a neck and shoulder massage for 15 minutes;
- Simply ask them how they're doing, and if they need anything. You'd be surprised at how far that simple sentiment can go;
- Give them extra time off when the proposal is complete;
- Thank them. Yes, simply thank them;
- Ask for their input as part of the debrief. You want to make them feel like they are contributing at a higher level;
- Bring them cupcakes (can you tell I like cupcakes? They just make me smile);
- Bring in a late-night bottle of wine if the team is working late (only one bottle, don't get too carried away!)
- Do team building activities outside of the office during down time

What else can you do?

The list is endless.

The most important thing here is to do something to appreciate your team.

You want them fresh, energetic and inspired when the next one hits your desk!

Back in my corporate days, we were working on a huge RFP response and of course we were down to crunch time. The crunch time wasn't because of the RFP team, it was because of senior leadership missing deadlines on their review.

The night before it needed to be shipped out, the RFP team was working well into the night to get this thing done. It included myself, someone from the production team, and an administrative assistant. At around 5:00pm, as everyone was leaving the office, we knew we were going to be there for quite a few more hours.

The Client Manager who was responsible for this proposal came by to let us know they were leaving. It was 5:00pm, they were certainly entitled, but the fact that we were going to be there late and they didn't even offer to help rubbed us all the wrong way. On top of that, I asked if we could expense dinner, and I was turned down.

Now, this was a multi-million-dollar RFP. There were three of us working way beyond business hours, not all of us getting paid for overtime, and you turn down a request for an expensed dinner that would have maybe cost $50?

Not cool. And none of us will ever forget that.

Now, I'd like to think that we still put our best foot forward, but no doubt we were frustrated and ticked. That energy is never good when you're wanting your team to put their best foot forward.

Take care of your team and they'll take care of you.

WATCH OUT FOR

6.11. Hidden Messages & Clues

There are a lot of hidden messages throughout an RFP if you pay close enough attention. Here are the main ones you should be looking for:

Their hot buttons - You may be able to recognize some hot buttons based on the way the RFP is written. If they continuously use one phrase throughout, or if they use all caps or bold font to emphasize a point, pay attention. These are likely areas where they've been burned which is why they are pointing them out in a strong manner. Make sure to address them in your response.

It's wired for someone else - A couple of indicators that it might be wired for someone else is if they don't have a bidder's conference or Q&A period, or if their response timeframe is unusually short. Another indicator is if they are asking for very specific expertise that only one company can provide.

They have no intention of hiring anyone, they're just gathering free information - Sometimes companies or entities use the RFP process to get free consulting. I wish I could say this doesn't happen, but it does. Some of the same things apply as above - unusually short timeframe, no Q&A period. You can also sometimes tell based on the questions that they ask or the vagueness of their contract timeline.

They're not the right fit for you - As you're working through the response, if you're feeling like the questions just aren't quite right, or if what they say they want is really far off base from what you believe they need, they might not be the right fit for you. If they are too negative, or too focused on low cost, or anything that pulls against your strategy, they might not be the right fit. Learn to recognize those signs and don't be afraid to pull the plug.

Now, with all that being said, hopefully you are also well tuned into your potential client through the relationship you've been working to build. Ideally, when you get the RFP you already have some background and you'll know the answers to these questions.

Realistically, I know that's not always going to happen. In that case, these tips on how to flush out those hidden messages and clues can help.

WATCH OUT FOR

6.12. Weak Words

There are certain words or phrases that, when used, diminish your credibility and power because they evoke weakness, or because they are overused. Here's a list of words that you should watch out for, depending on context. Many of them are unnecessary and can easily be removed or replaced.

"Typically"	"Periodic"	"If "	"Should"
"Maybe"	"Really"	"Try"	"We think"
"We believe"	"We feel"	"We hope"	"We'll try to"
"Very"	"Just"	"Actually"	"Obviously"
"Probably"	"Truly"	"Transparent"	

WATCH OUT FOR

6.13. Bad Writing

Yet another Obvious Chapters for the record books.

There's a lot of really bad writing going on out there. It's obvious based on the number of chapters (at least 20!) in this book that address writing in some way, shape or form.

Now, know that writing can be very subjective. Some people will love what you write, others will hate it. I'm not talking about that. I'm talking about the obvious parts of writing that you *should be* paying attention to.

I've addressed almost all of these in separate chapters along the way, and now they all come together under the category of bad writing:

- too "me" focused
- too much 'expert speak'
- too much fluff
- canned answers
- too vague
- not enough personality
- over-explanation
- under-explanation
- over-complication
- bad grammar – ugh!

Your response should be technical with a marketing spin, which I understand is hard to do. But truly, pay attention to each of these because they will bucket you into boring and unimaginative.

Boring and unimaginative don't sell.

WATCH OUT FOR

6.14. How You Ask Questions

Most every RFP either offers a bidder's conference or a written Q&A period. For public sector bids in particular, this is the only time you have to get clarification on the RFP.

It's key that you ask the right questions that are designed to get you the type of answer that you need.

Have you ever asked a question, and when the response came back you're even more confused than ever? Happens all the time. And most of the time it's because the question was crafted poorly. That's super-duper frustrating.

Here are some strategies to make sure you're asking the right types of questions:

- Avoid questions that will lead to a simple yes/no answer, unless you are truly wanting a yes/no response
- Ask with the end in mind; what type of an answer are you looking for? Then reverse engineer your question
- Avoid wide open questions such as, "please clarify..."; you need to ask them specifically what you need to know
- Reference the page number or section number
- Focus on questions that address the "what" or the "how"

Here are a couple of examples to help guide you:

Ask this: Please clarify whether Attachment C needs to be included for ALL bidders, or only if we are transferring signor authority to another entity?

Not this: Does Attachment C need to be included for all bidders?

The first one gives more context to why you are asking the question, so the buyer can understand why you are asking.

Ask this: Please clarify your definition of a published catalog. If we do not have a published catalog, will we be disqualified?

Not this: If we do not have a published catalog, will we be disqualified?

The first one asks for clarification on terminology so that when they come back with a yes/no answer on the disqualification question, there are no additional lingering questions.

No assumptions.

WATCH OUT FOR

6.15. Using A Winning Bid As A Model Bid

So often, companies will take a response that we won and use it as a "model" for future bids. Sure, maybe you're doing that because it has the most recent information. But watch out for the trap of doing that because you won with that proposal.

My team and I started working with a new client to help determine why they were losing RFPs. They'd had a string of painful losses and their morale was pretty low.

The first thing we did was a proposal review the proposal that they considered the "model proposal" since it was being used to populate other responses. As we reviewed this model proposal, we saw a lot of flaws. We went back to the client to ask for debrief notes and found that they never did a debrief. That model proposal was one that they had actually won so they didn't see a need to do a debrief.

We encouraged them to ask their client for the scoring sheets, and what we learned when we received them is that the only category that they scored high in was cost. They had two other competitors; one was disqualified, and the other was far too expensive. They won because of cost.

Further, we found that their scores in the other areas were not so great. So that content they were using for their model proposal was not so "model" after all.

Lesson learned: Just because you win with a response, doesn't mean it was a good response.

WATCH OUT FOR

6.16. Missed Requirements

It's crucial that you have someone assigned to manage the response, who is dedicated solely to making sure the requirements of the RFP are met.

Better yet, if you can have two sets of eyes on that, that's ideal. We are all human and we can miss things. It's another reason why you can't do this alone.

Early in my career with RFPs, I was managing the response for the consulting firm that I worked for. I went through the proposal with a fine-tooth comb – or so I thought.

Of course we were on a tight timeframe. I read through the Scope of Work, I combed through the Response Requirements, I put together our response template and went to work populating it.

There was a point where I thought, this just seems too easy. Their questions were pretty high level and very straight forward. Wow, what a great RFP!

It wasn't until one of the other consultants asked me a question that sent me into a complete panic mode. We were a day away from our draft needing to be completed, and because of this question, I realized there was a whole detailed section that I had overlooked. It was tucked between the terms and conditions and some required forms, not even close to the Scope of Work section. I went from having ten questions to answer, to having over 150 questions to answer.

I pulled it out, thankfully. I worked into the wee hours of the morning to get that done, I tapped into prior responses that provided some answers, and there were a couple of other key folks that were kind enough to help out. Together we were able to answer all of the additional questions. But whew, that was close, and I will never forget it. (and now nor will you)

Look, we're human. We miss things. It's great to have more than one person who is good at attention to detail looking over the requirements to make sure they are met. It's heartbreaking to get disqualified because you missed a simple requirement. And generally, there are some pretty upset team members looking to lay blame when that happens.

The Snapshot

Key Takeaways

This section isn't here to scare you. Well, maybe it is. But it's more to make you aware. These are things that I see all the time. Buyers tell me they see these things all the time. Most of them are easily fixed. Pay attention and keep an eye out so you don't make these mistakes.

Resources

Download your free RFP Success™ Kit to access:

- The Response Calendar Template
- The Checks and Balances Checklist

Chapter 7.

The Ninja Warrior, Pro-Only Tricks To Up Your RFP Game

I don't care how long you've been doing this, there is always room for improvement. In fact, I was having dinner with an old friend and she was telling me how great they were at responding to RFPs, they had a pretty high win percentage. As we got talking, I was tossing out some of my tips and strategies and she had several "a-ha" moments. Heck, I still learn from clients and colleagues every day.

There's always room for improvement. What can you do to up level your responses? Read on, I am confident you'll be able to take away a few nuggets.

7.1. Consider The Reviewers' Personality Styles

When we respond to RFPs, we make a lot of incorrect assumptions about the reviewers on the other end. As I've addressed in other chapters, this may not be conscious, but because we are so entrenched in *our* response and *our* challenges we don't always slow down long enough to realize that there are real dynamic beings on the other side of the RFP. This oversight is especially prevalent when working with public sector proposals.

We are so entrenched in our response and our challenges we don't always slow down long enough to realize that there are real dynamic beings on the other side of the RFP.

There is likely more than one person evaluating a proposal, and each one comes with their own uniqueness. They have different perspectives and different personalities.

Let's talk about the four major behavioral categories (aka personalities) that people generally fall into:

The Straight-Shooter – the Straight Shooter doesn't like to waste time. They're likely the ones that will read your Tier One answer and then move on. They like efficient and they are generally very direct. They like to do business with people who don't waste their time and can get results. Straight Shooters love case studies and quantifiable results.

Social Butterfly - the Social Butterfly loves people and they are generally very outgoing and extroverted. Reality Rich is definitely a Social Butterfly. They want to do business with people who they like. They do NOT like boring and will appreciate getting to know someone through personal stories and connecting to their passion. They will also likely just read the Tier One answer (just like Reality Rich!).

Slow 'n Steady - The Slow 'n Steady is very methodical and likes process. They will appreciate responses that break things out into steps. They are generally very loyal and once they trust you, they likely won't want to leave you.

Statistical - you guessed it, the Statistical personality loves data. They tend to be very analytical and they don't like fluff. You can easily lose their attention in an RFP response if you're telling too many stories without the data to back them up.

So how do you balance *all* of these personalities in one response? You combine a little bit of everything, and don't do too much of one thing. Understanding the personality styles and how to sell to each one is something we cover in The RFP Success™ Institute as a separate training, it's that important. And it's one of the reasons that I suggest tiering your answers into the three different levels (if you missed that one, go back to pg. 91. You'll capture something for everyone.

7.2. Tell Them What They Don't Know

This can get a little tricky, so please don't confuse this with over-selling and over-sharing.

There is a time and place for telling them what they don't know, and that time and place is in your response *only if* it is relevant and important to the solution at hand. This is not an upsell or cross-sell situation, it's more of a value-add.

Did they overlook something that is necessary for the success of the project? Make sure you include that without being condescending.

Don't overwhelm,
don't give them too much.

But this is an opportunity for you to show your expertise in an area that would set you apart from your competition. When you tell them something they don't even know they don't know, that gives them pause, you're upping the game.

A recent example was a proposal that a client was doing for a hard-to-unseat incumbent contract. They knew they had a competitive advantage because of the insider knowledge they had with a governing agency that approves or disapproves funding for the prospect. It was easy for us to point out several things that the governing agency looks for, without giving it all away. It was enough to educate the prospect and get them intrigued about working with my client because of that knowledge.

You don't want to give away the farm in an RFP, but you do want to "tease" your knowledge and experience when you know it's fresh and unfamiliar.

7.3. Apply The Skim Test

If the reviewers were to just do a quick skim of your proposal – much like hungover Reality Rich would do – what would they see?

If they only have 15 minutes to thumb through your response, what message would they get?

Would they know what your Proposal Promise is? Would there be some key points that stand out? Would they be visually drawn in? Would there be something that would cause them to want to read more?

Would they get enough from your headers, and your compliance grid, and your call-outs to make an informed decision?

Would they see a lot of white space with some colorful and interesting graphics that would draw them in?

Every single proposal should go through the skim test. You may have to build in some extra time for this, but it is well worth it. And since you're open to embracing change in the process (hint hint), it's totally doable!

7.4. Address The Elephant In The Room

We've all had that one proposal where we meet 98% of the criteria, but there's this one task that we aren't quite well-versed in.

If it's small enough, you can probably speak to what you know and move on. But many times, it's best to address it head on and turn it into a positive. When you avoid it, it will likely come across as if you're trying to hide something.

If you don't meet a requirement and you are still choosing to bid, you're better off addressing the fact that you don't meet the requirement. Figure out how to turn it into a positive or showcase how you can overcome it. You never, ever want to lie. That will come back and bite you.

For example: Let's say your company doesn't have experience in one particular area and you have to bring in an independent contractor. Your competitor is aware of this, and they are going to use that as an advantage and a differentiator, claiming that because they have all staff in-house, it will be easier to manage and control. That's okay, let them claim that. For you, you need to claim why hiring an independent contractor is actually a *better* thing. It could be because they specialize in just that, so they are heads and tails above anyone that you could hire into your organization.

Whatever the elephant is, claim it and own it, and talk to the benefits of it. Don't sweep it under the carpet and try to hide it.

7.5. Take Some Risks

There's a time and place for taking risks and you need to know what that looks like for you. Surprise surprise, this goes back to having a strategy and knowing your green-light clients (wink wink).

Here are a couple of times where you should pull out all the stops and take some risks:

- When you're trying to unseat an incumbent. It is hard to do, but it can be done. You're going to have to show why it's worth it, so now is the time to take some risks.
- When you're looking to get into a new market or offering. Sometimes the risk is bidding low and "buying" the business; other times the risk is being incredibly bold in your approach and proposal promise.

These are calculated, strategic risks, not "blindly jumping off a cliff" risks.

Risks that are really going to stand out to get the buyers' attention when you might otherwise blend into the background or be dismissed.

7.6. Don't Underestimate Objectivity

"You can't see the picture when you're inside the frame."
-Les Brown, Motivational Speaker

That is one of my favorite quotes because there is so much truth to it.

This is another reason why you can't do it all yourself. You can't put together the entire proposal, and then have the ability to look at it objectively.

Why is objectivity so important?

Because you want to make sure you're not missing anything, or making mistakes, or speaking the wrong language. Having an objective perspective gives you clarity and will help with your positioning.

Having some objectivity to review what you're doing will help you continue to up-level your game.

I don't care if you have a dedicated team of twenty proposal professionals, they work on this over and over again. They can no longer see their responses objectively.

> *A client engaged us to review a proposal they were submitting to a local school district. They had submitted many proposals in an attempt to get their foot in the door with this school district. They were determined.*

Unfortunately, they ran out of time to have us do our complete review. What we did instead is a high level cursory review to give her tips that could make the biggest immediate impact.

She incorporated about five key things that we suggested. It wasn't as much as we would have liked, but we knew it would make a difference.

She won the contract!

I tell you this story to emphasize that even small changes can make a huge difference in how your proposal reads.

When my team and I conduct Proposal Reviews we're looking at things with those objectivity glasses, and we're looking for all of the things that I've talked about in this book. Things like:

- Are you answering the questions? Are you actually providing an answer to the specific question that they asked?
- Are you focusing on the solution?
- Do you have your Proposal Promise clearly stated throughout the proposal?
- Are you adding personality? Or is your response boring?
- Can we understand your response and what it will be like to work with you?

When you're too close to it, it's hard to see those things from an objective viewpoint. You should always have someone review the response for objectivity that hasn't been involved in the writing for the biggest impact.

7.7. Plant Seeds Of Doubt

This is a powerful strategy particularly when you're trying to unseat an incumbent or stand out above your competition.

This is not about manipulation, but rather the opportunity to ensure that your potential client is considering all angles.

When you have a competitive advantage, your ability to plant seeds of doubt will help you seal the deal.

The best way to plant seeds of doubt is to ask questions. These questions target specific areas that you know *only* your company can address.

To craft these questions, consider this: Are there certain competitive advantages that only you have? If so, then you'll want to ask a question in your proposal that forces the buyer to not only question whether they would get that same thing from another vendor, but also question how they've lived without that for so long.

Here are a couple of examples of recent questions that we used to plant some seeds of doubt for a client proposal:

- Are you confident that you are getting the most out of your {vendor} using {this} as a tool?
- Is your current vendor quantifying how their efficiencies are affecting your bottom line?

When you ask these types of questions, you have to *know* what the answers will be. That's where the power lies.

7.8. Bid When You Know You'll Lose

Please read this carefully and don't just take that title and run with it.

Sometimes, you may want to bid even if you know you'll lose.

What??! Sounds crazy, right?

There is a strategy to this.

The main reason you'd want to do this is if there is an incumbent who has the current contract, and you don't know of any ill-will or problems with that incumbent. However, you have identified this entity as a green light target and you want to start building the relationship and getting your name in front of the prospect.

This is a long-term play. Don't do this without understanding the impact on your business, and don't do this if it's not part of your bigger business development strategy.

A client made the strategic decision to bid on a project that had a current vendor that their prospect was very happy with. They knew it was a long shot, but this prospect was at the top of their green-light list and strategically it made sense to bid.

Two weeks after the decision was made, our client received a call from their prospect asking them to come in to present on a smaller piece of work that would have been a conflict of interest for the winning bidder.

If our client hadn't bid, they wouldn't have gotten that call. Sure, it was a smaller piece of business, but it got them in their door which was their ultimate goal.

7.9. Apply General Marketing Principles

These marketing principles have been addressed in other chapters above but bear repeating all together. They are that important.

You are indeed marketing and selling through your RFP response – sales and marketing go hand in hand folks!

So go ahead, apply these principles and see how well they improve your responses!

Don't confuse your reader - A confused mind doesn't buy. Avoid jargon, industry speak, techie speak, big words, big sentences, and anything else that can confuse the reader. Keep it simple, speak to every level, and don't confuse with big words or complicated explanations. Reality Rich gets confused easily, so be careful!

You have 2-3 seconds to make an impression – the world is a busy place and we have more information and noise than ever. You only have 2 to 3 seconds to make a good first impression, make it count.

By the way, this used to be 7 to 10 seconds; the world's-a-changing!

People have to hear something up to 7 times before it really resonates - don't assume that because you've said it once, that it has sunk in. Likely not.

Write to an 8th grade level - All the big papers and magazines use this rule of thumb; some even write to a fourth-grade level. It's meant to ensure understanding and to keep it simple so we can easily consume the information.

Nobody cares about you (WIIFT) - focus on What's In It For Them, not *you*. Outcome over ego.

Make it pretty and friendly - Enough said.

Want more marketing and sales tips? These up leveling tactics are in The RFP Success™ Institute, where we go in depth with marketing and sales tips and training because it's so important to the readability of your proposals. Don't be afraid to embrace and integrate marketing concepts!

❑ Don't Just Take My Word For It...

When I decided to ask experts to contribute their genius to this book, my good friend and colleague Arlene Pedersen was one of the first people I thought of. Arlene is brilliant at making businesses look good – from the visual to the words they use to describe what they do. Her company, Be Freaking Awesome, says it all!

***

No matter what you are selling, the more you resonate with your potential customers, the higher your success. Proposals are the gateway to longstanding relationships and income, and your company's message and brand has the ability to create instant trust and credibility. By not expressing that message powerfully and succinctly – you will drown in a sea of RFP mediocrity.

After two decades in the branding and messaging world, I know this to be true more than ever. I cut my teeth responding to RFPs in the development world and remember a fatal mistake that is often overlooked.

PEOPLE actually review them.

Committee members are reading multiple proposals, many of which are repeating the same promises. Without creating something extraordinary or FREAKING Authentic & Memorable, yours could be cast into the "round filing cabinet". To prevent this, here are three of my longstanding best practices that will help you up your game on a whole new level.

Be REAL.

You are going to be working with other humans when you win your RFPs, so start sounding like one! Weave in your company values, philosophy and ethics in a subtle and artful way. Have your team players bios written in a way that they are capable and fascinating – for whatever their interests are. Your RFP should FEEL like your company culture and what it is like to work with you.

Are you passionate about philanthropic giving or volunteering? Look for ways in which you share values to create a connection - price can sometimes be eliminated as a barrier when your value and values resonate with your customers. That is a beautiful thing.

Are you at a disadvantage in some way? Look at those objections that the buyer might have and demonstrate how you navigate those and show social proof to support it. Do not ignore the elephant in the room; face it head on, powerfully.

Be Digestible.

Seriously, this is one of the most common marketing mistakes I see out there. Turn off the fire hose - make it digestible and skim-able to make it enjoyable to read. Ditch long, dense paragraphs and pull out snappy key phrases to express your philosophy or values to give a favorable first impression.

Your RFP should be visibly appealing. For high-end corporate proposals, it should look like beautiful magazine - gorgeous pro photos if you can. For public sector proposals, use thematic stock images to demonstrate concepts when you can. In any case, have critical information formatted in a consistent and easy to access manner and include a thoughtful balance between paragraphs, statements and imagery. Seeding social proof throughout the document is a must – highlight testimonials to address objections before they show up, as well as other testimonials; wins or awards create a compound effect of your client's love for you.

Be FREAKING Awesome.

Quality brands are EVERYWHERE, you will be judged on yours so look like you are in-it-to-win-it. Hire professionals where appropriate – for example, an experienced graphic designer or a messenger/editor to make your proposal potent. Is there a theme you can use as a metaphor for your main message to use on your cover and throughout your proposal? Keep the design clean with plenty of "breathing" space with a main message visible within the first 2 seconds on each page. If you are looking at each page like you don't want to read it, or it occurs overwhelming, chances are someone else will feel the same.

Yes, a theme! I couldn't agree more!

Being more of your Freaking Awesome selves in your proposals takes some courage but will make you memorable and attractive to do business with. People buy emotionally and need to justify it with logic – by you finding a way to resonate with potential customers through your proposals, you will win more RFPs and will work with people you'll love.

Arlene S. Pedersen, CEO
Be Freaking Awesome

***

Thanks Arlene! It's 'freaking awesome' (see how I did that??) how in-line your words are with so many of the messages sprinkled throughout the book. Spot. On.

If you're part of The RFP Success™ Institute, make sure you check out our design gallery for some fun and creative ideas to add punch to your proposals!

7.10. Get Creative

This is particularly true in the private sector, but don't discount it in the public sector. You may have to be a bit more careful and low key in the public sector, but your readers still like creativity.

Your competitors are all probably being boring in their public-sector proposals too, so adding some creativity will definitely help you stand out.

Here are some ideas for creativity:

- Embed video, either explaining a specific process, or introducing the team
- Take a team photo with the key team members –make it a fun photo, not a snoozer.
- For commercial proposals, you can generally get much more creative by sending something representative of your company along with the proposal. If you didn't see some of the creativity that went with the Amazon HQ2 proposals (hey, one city in Arizona went so far as to send a live cactus!), it's worth doing a quick search to check it out. Of course, that's a bit over the top, but it was a "go big or go home" type of opportunity.
- We used to send chocolate telephones along with some of our proposals with a note that said, "Give us a call to discuss our proposal further." It often resulted in a phone call!

- A couple of other creative approaches for the Amazon HQ2 included Birmingham, Alabama who set up large Amazon boxes and giant replicas of Amazon's Dash Buttons all around town; and Stonecrest, Georgia who offered to rename itself to Amazon, Georgia if they won. Talk about creativity!
- Turn your proposal into a magazine, with beautiful professional graphics and a creative layout

Creativity will most definitely stand out.

Inject more relative to the proposal you're submitting

7.11. Never, Ever Skip The Final Look Review

My colleague Amy Shuman gave some great advice (pg. 41):

Never, ever skip the final look review.

A final look review is post-production, whether electronic or hard copy. It's when you thumb through the entire response to make sure that everything is included, the bound copy is in order, all electronic files are included and openable, things like that. It's that final look right before you box it up for delivery (or press the send button).

When time is tight, this is one thing that can easily get pushed aside. You just want to get it out the door -- certainly everything is fine -- and the delivery truck is arriving any minute. You have just run out of time to get this done.

It seems harmless but let me tell you a story.....

I had a colleague tell me a story about their most heart-breaking proposal submittal. They had a high-profile client and they were bidding on an extension of some work they had been doing. They had been working for years to position themselves well for this project.

The competition was stiff but they felt confident in their proposal promise and their relationship. They pulled together a top-notch response team, they strategized, they stayed on task, and they put together a response that they were very proud of.

They even built in enough time to get all of the appropriate reviews done. Even the final look review.

Their mistake? They only did a final look of the master copy. But there were five duplicate copies that also had to be submitted. Turns out, all of the copies were screwed up. Somehow during production, things got swapped out, pages got turned around. It was such a mess that they got disqualified because most of the reviewers weren't able to review it. Ouch!

You just absolutely, positively need to make enough time for this. These are the type of stories that are so heartbreaking, and that you never really get over when you're involved. It's much too much time and energy to lose for something like that. And trust me when I say, Reality Rich doesn't like disqualifying you any more than you like being disqualified.

Build in the time for that final look, and don't ever compromise on it.

7.12. Become Certified

If you are a small business and have a level of disadvantage, you may qualify as a disadvantaged business enterprise. If you qualify, becoming a small diverse business through certification can help you win more contracts and get noticed in the marketplace.

The certification comes into play in both public and private sector. Government entities have small-business set-aside contracts, where many large corporations have supplier diversity programs that support small disadvantaged business entities.

Warning! Be careful not to get too starry-eye here though – this needs to be part of your overall strategy and you've got to be realistic.

Things won't happen for you overnight. In fact, I was having a conversation recently with a certified women business enterprise, and she told me she was just starting to get traction with her certification after being certified for almost three years.

I had another conversation with someone who decided she'd get certified because part of her current year plan was to get more public-sector business. I had to be the one to break the news that she likely wouldn't see a return on her certification in the current year, particularly on the federal side. Yes, you can get lucky, but who wants to rely on luck?!

It's a long-term play, just like any of the big opportunities and relationships are. You have to work it. It's not a magic pill.

❑ Don't Just Take My Word For It...

Meet Heather Cox, President of Certify My Company. Heather is an expert in the area of diverse business certification, and she's here to give you the lay of the land so you can determine if certification is right for you!

***

Diverse Business Certification; is it for you?

Consumers have a plethora of choices when selecting a service or product provider, so a differentiated marketing strategy is a key to business success. One vital way to differentiate yourself from the pack is by certifying your woman-, minority- LGBT- Veteran – or Disabled owned company as a business that meets the exact criteria of key certifying organizations. You can reap many rewards through this certification by contracting or partnering on projects with other certified businesses, and by becoming a potential bidder on corporate and public agency contracts who are specifically looking for these types of certification.

Certification gives diverse owned businesses opportunities to become part of corporate and governmental supply chains.

Supply chain is just a fancy way to say sales channel.

Given the rapidly changing demographic of the United States, Corporate America is seeking ways in which to have its employee and supplier base reflect the population. Diverse owned businesses are often more cost-effective and offer an expanded customer base and market share for the corporations who contract with them. Diversity-owned businesses tend to have greater access to emerging markets and make outstanding contributions to the economic viability of the communities in which they are located. Certification is one means in which Corporate America has chosen to achieve these goals.

There is an abundance of certification options, and it is important to be sure to choose the certification that will most benefit your company. For the purposes of this section I am going to focus on the certifications that the Fortune 1000 community prefer.

1. *Women's Business Enterprise National Council (WBENC) certifies woman business enterprises (WBE);*

2. *National Minority Supplier Development Council (NMSDC) certifies minority business enterprises (MBE);*

3. *National Gay and Lesbian Chamber of Commerce (NGLCC) certifies LGBT business enterprises (LGBTBE);*

4. *US Business Leadership Network (USBLN) certifies disabled business enterprises and service disabled veteran owned businesses (DOBE, V-DOB and SDV-DOBE);*

5. *National Veteran Business Development Council (NVBDC) certifies veteran and service disabled owned veteran business enterprises (VOBE and SDVOBE).*

These are what I refer to as the Big 5.

Certification for all 5 organizations has 3 main requirements:

1. **Ownership.** *Is the company owned 51% or more by 1 or more people of the diversity demographic being certified?*

2. **Operation.** *Are the diversity people for which the certification relies upon involved in the day to day operation and does one or more hold the highest-ranking title.*

3. **Control.** *Does the diverse person/people have ultimate control of the company as stated in the company's governing documents?*

Now before you get any funny ideas about trying to trick the system... DON'T! The big 5 certification organizations have gone to great lengths to weed out any ineligible companies and companies thinking they will simply change the ownership paperwork! They are smart, and your name and reputation can be tarnished should you attempt such deception.

However, if your company is eligible it can be a fantastic marketing tool and differentiator that can be the piece that tips the scales in your favor in an RFP or bid process.

Heather Cox, President
Certify My Company

***

Heather, you are a wealth of amazing certification information. And thanks for taking on this arduous process for us certified business owners who don't have the time or energy to tackle it on our own!

7.13. Checks and Balances

Once you have your RFP drafted, going through and doing a thorough readability review of the proposal is very important. This is *on top of* a solid editorial review.

These ten checks and balances questions are essential to increasing your potential for winning. If you can honesty answer YES to these questions, you'll be well on your way to success. (And yes, we have a pretty pdf for this in your Kit.)

1. Have you actually answered the questions? Have you answered all parts of each question?
2. Do you 'smack 'em between the eyes' at least 7 times with your proposal promise?
3. Are you consistent with your terminology throughout the response? Have you removed any reference to another company or entity?
4. Are you talking more about the solution you provide to *their* want/need and less about you?
5. Have you added value beyond price?
6. Have you fully and truly differentiated yourself?
7. Have you met all the requirements of the RFP?
8. Have you addressed what they will be evaluating you on, with more emphasis on the areas that will be scored the highest?

9. Have you done enough to keep your readers engaged? Have you removed the bore and injected personality?

10. Are your answers Simple, Specific and Succinct?

Very few companies will create the draft far enough in advance to go through this checklist, but it can make all the difference for your success. Build in one extra day and make this happen and you'll have a winning submittal!

The Snapshot

Key Takeaways

The work of improving our RFP responses is never done. Even if you have all the basics down, your team is a well-oiled machine, there are always new ways to kick it up a notch or two. Get creative, don't fall into a rut. Find new ways to inject interest and exposure for your company.

Resources

Don't forget to download The RFP Success™ Kit for your Checks and Balances checklist (http://RFPSuccess.expert/kit).

You can also access the design gallery on The RFP Success™ Institute (http://RFPSuccessInstitute.com).

And make sure you check out the Big 5 Certification Organizations that Expert Contributor, Heather Cox mentions:

1. *Women's Business Enterprise National Council (WBENC) certifies woman business enterprises (WBE);*

2. *National Minority Supplier Development Council (NMSDC) certifies minority business enterprises (MBE);*

3. *National Gay and Lesbian Chamber of Commerce (NGLCC) certifies LGBT business enterprises (LGBTBE);*

4. *US Business Leadership Network (USBLN) certifies disabled business enterprises and service disabled veteran owned businesses (DOBE, V-DOB and SDV-DOBE);*

5. *National Veteran Business Development Council (NVBDC) certifies veteran and service disabled owned veteran business enterprises (VOBE and SDVOBE).*

Conclusion

Creating a winning RFP Success™ Strategy starts with having a great mindset, creating both a business and bidding strategy, developing simple yet effective processes, and building those relationships. Those are the basic essentials. Yes, I said essentials. At least if you want to win.

From there, you have to add personality, avoid the crazy mistakes, treat the readers like human beings (that's why I included Reality Rich!), and SMACK 'em between the eyes to get your point across in a busy, bustling world.

And remember, even though an RFP is a written response to prescribed questions, make no mistake, you are indeed Marketing and Selling your services. Treat it as such.

Want more?

Download the RFP Success™ Kit here: http://RFPSuccess.expert/kit.

A Million Thanks

What's a book without the people who helped make it happen?!

We can't do it alone, we shouldn't even try. People want to help and if you have the right people in your corner, they will step up to the plate and enthusiastically say "Yes!"

Expert Contributors, thank you. Your willingness to tell your story and share your knowledge with my readers means a lot!

Talmar Anderson, Hiring & Management Expert, Boss Actions
Heather Cox, President, Certify My Company
Arlene S. Pedersen, CEO, Be Freaking Awesome
Amy Schuman, National Marketing Director, Myers and Stauffer LC
Tish Times, CEO, Tish Times Networking & Sales Training

Robin Merritt, even after knowing what you know about me from our college days, you still believe in me! Thank you for your continued support and for your enthusiasm in writing the Forward to this book. Not because we're friends, but because you really liked the book.

And **Ali Craig**, YOU ROCK! Publisher and Branding Expert extraordinaire, you have made this a better book. Your insight and vision amped it up a few degrees. Forever grateful.

About the Author

Seven times author, Lisa Rehurek is passionate about helping businesses succeed by mastering the "Request For Proposal" process - aka RFPs. Bringing her 25+ years of RFP experience to her clients, Lisa's work has garnered results such as an 80% improved proposal win rate, over 70% revenue growth, and a 28% decrease in employee turnover. Lisa is a consultant on RFP optimization for many corporate and government clients across the nation. She has also trained on RFP success for many groups including the SBLA (Salt River Project and ASU's Small Business Leadership Academy) and WBEC-West. In addition to speaking and training around the country on how any organization can have RFP Success™, her RFP Success Institute™ helps businesses - large and small - improve their RFP results through simple but powerful training, tools and templates.

Lisa resides in Tempe, Arizona with her two beloved pups Duke and Oliver.

CPSIA information can be obtained
at www.ICGtesting.com
Printed in the USA
LVOW10*2356020518
575739LV00001BA/1/P